# MANKIND

## MIDDLE ENGLISH TEXTS SERIES

The Middle English Texts Series is designed for classroom use. Its goal is to make available to teachers and students texts that occupy an important place in the literary and cultural canon but have not been readily available in student editions. The series does not include those authors, such as Chaucer, Langland, or Malory, whose English works are normally in print in good student editions. The focus is, instead, upon Middle English literature adjacent to those authors that teachers need in compiling the syllabuses they wish to teach. The editions maintain the linguistic integrity of the original work but within the parameters of modern reading conventions. The texts are printed in the modern alphabet and follow the practices of modern capitalization, word formation, and punctuation. Manuscript abbreviations are silently expanded, and *u/v* and *j/i* spellings are regularized according to modern orthography. Yogh (ȝ) is transcribed as *g, gh, y*, or *s*, according to the sound in Modern English spelling to which it corresponds; thorn (þ) and eth (ð) are transcribed as *th*. Distinction between the second person pronoun and the definite article is made by spelling the one *thee* and the other *the*, and final *-e* that receives full syllabic value is accented (e.g., *charité*). Hard words, difficult phrases, and unusual idioms are glossed on the page, either in the right margin or at the foot of the page. Explanatory and textual notes appear at the end of the text, often along with a glossary. The editions include short introductions on the history of the work, its merits and points of topical interest, and brief working bibliographies.

This series is published in association with the University of Rochester.

Medieval Institute Publications is a program of
The Medieval Institute, College of Arts and Sciences

WESTERN MICHIGAN UNIVERSITY

# MANKIND

Edited by
Kathleen M. Ashley and Gerard NeCastro

TEAMS • Middle English Texts Series

MEDIEVAL INSTITUTE PUBLICATIONS
Western Michigan University
*Kalamazoo*

Copyright © 2010 by the Board of Trustees of
Western Michigan University

Printed and bound by CPI Group (UK) Ltd, Croydon, CR0 4YY

**Library of Congress Cataloging-in-Publication Data**

Mankind (Morality play)
  Mankind / edited by Kathleen M. Ashley and Gerard NeCastro.
    p. cm. -- (Middle English texts series)
  "Published for TEAMS (The Consortium for the Teaching of the Middle Ages) in
association with the University of Rochester."
  Includes bibliographical references.
  ISBN 978-1-58044-140-7 (pbk. : alk. paper)
  1. Mankind (Fictitious character)--Drama. 2. Moralities, English. I. Ashley,
Kathleen M., 1944- II. NeCastro, Gerard. III. Title.
  PR1261.M3 2010
  822'.2--dc22

                          2009050468

ISBN 978-1-58044-140-7

P  5  4  3  2  1

# ❧ Contents

 # ACKNOWLEDGMENTS

I am grateful to all my students at the University of Southern Maine over the years who read *Mankind*, responded with astonishment to the play, and expressed enthusiastic appreciation for medieval drama in general. Special thanks must go to Davidson College students George Vahamikos, Marianne Snow, and Mariana De Fede for their work in an Independent Study course on *Mankind*. Their careful research on the critical literature and thoughtful suggestions for the glossing and notes have contributed immeasurably to this edition. Thanks also to Clair Berrin of Oxford University, who has generously supplied bibliography on the historical references in the play from her own researches.

—Kathleen M. Ashley


I would like to thank my many students at the University of Maine at Machias, whose comments, ideas, and performances have shaped this edition. Likewise, I wish to thank the Chaucer Studio for its 2007 staged reading of the play, as it illuminated several of the most difficult passages in the play. I would also like to express my gratitude to the many visitors to From Stage to Page without whose appreciation all my editing would be in vain. Naturally, I am fully indebted to "my suavius solas and synguler recreatory."

—Gerard NeCastro


We also wish to thank Russell A. Peck and his advisory board for including *Mankind* in the Middle English Texts Series. Leah Haught at the University of Rochester has been our point person. She formatted the text, checked the edition against the manuscript and other modern editions, and compiled many of the textual notes. Russell Peck gave the finished manuscript a careful reading and added a few explanatory notes. The volume was read in Rochester by John H. Chandler and Kathryn D. Van Wert and at the press by Patricia Hollahan and Tom Krol. Finally, we are all grateful to the National Endowment of the Humanities for their continuing support of METS.

# Introduction by Kathleen M. Ashley

*Mankind* is without a doubt the most amusing and controversial morality play surviving from fifteenth-century England. As an allegory about the vulnerable situation in which most people find themselves — torn between good judgment and the temptation to misbehave — the play's moral action is conventional. Its theological message that God's mercy is available to even the most abysmal sinner until the moment of death is likewise totally orthodox.[1] However, the predictable seriousness of the subject is balanced and complicated by the high jinks of four disreputable characters (Mischief, New Guise, Nowadays, and Nought), who symbolize worldly temptation, and by the sensational tricks of the demonic Titivillus, who manages to seduce the Mankind character into sin. Against the pious rhetoric of the chief good character Mercy, the Worldlings and Titivillus send a barrage of teasing wit, nonsense patter, and outright lies that lead Mankind astray and simultaneously entertain the audience. The striking presence of popular dramatic modes has generated considerable scholarly debate, but *Mankind* is now widely accepted as the most theatrically effective early English play.[2]

## Staging

According to David Bevington, *Mankind* epitomizes the kind of play in the repertory of a traveling troupe of actors and may represent the beginnings of popular professional drama in England.[3] Unlike another well-known fifteenth-century morality play, the *Castle of Perseverance* (which has a huge cast and is designed for place-and-scaffold staging), *Mankind* would require only six actors and limited costumes and props. Bevington argues that one actor could play the parts of both Mercy and Titivillus, who are never on stage at the same time — a technique of "doubling" commonly used by sixteenth-century troupes before the establishment of permanent theaters in London. Props called for are mundane and portable: a rosary, a flute, a spade, a writing implement and paper, a noose, fetters, a board, a bag of seed, a scourge for

---

[1] Robert Potter's *English Morality Play* provides a comprehensive introduction to the theological and dramatic traditions that defined the morality genre.

[2] Speaking of late medieval morality plays in the tradition of "English theatricality," Stanton B. Garner, Jr. says "these plays are aware of their own existence in performance, draw upon performance in various ways, and in fact constitute some of the most sophisticated artistic and moral explorations of theatricality in English drama" ("Theatricality in *Mankind* and *Everyman*," p. 273). On *Mankind*'s "metatheatricality," see also Twycross, "Theatricality of Medieval English Plays," p. 73.

[3] Bevington, *From Mankind to Marlowe*, pp. 8–25.

Mercy, a large-headed mask[4] and a net for the devil, stolen goods, and several jackets of different lengths.[5] *Mankind* also contains the first evidence of commercial support for theater, a scene (lines 459–72) in which the Worldlings collect money from the audience to bring on the chief attraction, the devil Titivillus.

Since we have no information about actual productions of *Mankind*, critics have speculated about its staging based on details in the text. References to a "hostler" and "tapester" and the play's bawdy language first led to the suggestion that it might have been performed in an inn or on a stage set up in an innyard for a rustic village audience.[6] However, the presence of liturgical language and puns on Latin words indicate venues where the audience included the literate classes — such as the private hall of a rural manor house,[7] religious guild,[8] or college. Tom Pettitt argues that references to "this house" (line 209), the exit at a "dore" (line 159), and the crowding of the audience around the acting area "suggest indoor performance, perhaps in the great Hall of a domestic or institutional residence."[9] Mercy's address to two classes of spectators — "ye soverens that sytt and ye brothern that stonde ryght uppe" (line 29) — likewise suggests a diverse audience. Perhaps the most plausible conclusion is that *Mankind* is a play whose appeal cuts across class lines and social categories and could therefore be produced in a wide variety of settings.

FESTIVE ENTERTAINMENT

Despite its portability and wide appeal, the play's themes and allusions associate it with a particular time of year: the pre-Lenten season. During this winter period of variable length that stretched from Epiphany (January 6) to the beginning of Lent at Ash Wednesday four to six weeks later, carnivalesque activities were common throughout Europe. Carnival authorized the free expression of the "grotesque body" theorized by Bakhtin — a body "unruly, excre-

---

[4] The fact that the devil Titivillus is masked would make it easier to have the same actor play the parts of both Mercy and Titivillus, as Meg Twycross and Sarah Carpenter point out (*Masks and Masking*, p. 243).

[5] Typical of the allegorical morality genre, *Mankind* uses images of clothing to represent the state of the soul. As Mankind falls into worldly sin he discards his farmer's robe for increasingly brief jackets which symbolize not only the "new gyse" of fashion but also frivolous youth; see Tony Davenport, "Lusty fresche galaunts."

[6] See Bevington, *Mankind to Marlowe*, p. 15, and Smart, "Some Notes on *Mankind*," pp. 306–08. The play's language drew scabrous attacks from late nineteenth and early twentieth century scholars like Hardin Craig, who called it a "very badly degenerated version of what was once a typical morality" ("Morality Plays and Elizabethan Drama," p. 69); and a "play of the utmost ignorance and crudity" performed by players "whose appeal was to the uneducated and vulgar" (*English Religious Drama of the Middle Ages*, p. 350). According to E. K. Chambers, the play exhibits a "very degraded type of morality aiming at entertainment rather than edification" (*English Literature at the Close of the Middle Ages*, pp. 61–62). A. P. Rossiter calls it "a dirty play written for inn-yard amusement" (*English Drama*, p. 107), and Arnold Williams suggests it seizes "every chance for irrelevant low comedy, so that the tone of the piece is now that of the burlesque theater or the lower sort of music hall" (*Drama of Medieval England*, p. 156).

[7] Clopper, "*Mankind* and Its Audience."

[8] Marshall, "'O Ye Soverens that Sytt and Ye Brothern that Stonde Ryght Wppe.'"

[9] Pettitt, "*Mankind*: An English *Fastnachtspiel*?" p. 191.

mental, rude, and unregulated" and "crudely rebellious," terms that describe the vice figures in *Mankind*.[10] The Mediterranean countries celebrated Carnival, Germany and Scandinavia had *Fastnacht* or *fastelavn*, while in England Shrovetide (the three days before Ash Wednesday) was celebrated with special foods, cock-fighting, and football games.[11] The boisterous games of the Worldlings (New Guise, Nowadays, and Nought) in *Mankind* call to mind such seasonal amusements, including the invitation to play football (line 732), while their extensive scatological fooling would not be out of place in a Carnival play.

There are also motifs recognizable from winter Mummers' plays, including cries to the audience to "make space," the deliberately teasing buildup to the entrance of the devil Titivillus with his big head, the *quête* or taking of a collection at the moment of greatest excitement,[12] the mock beheading and castration of the three Worldlings and their mock curing by Mischief, as well as the offer of "game" or performance that includes comic song, dance, and "ribald repartee."[13] Finally, there is the absurd and improvisational patter of the vice figures, which suggests to Richard Axton the "nonsensical, gnomic quality of the folk-play idiom."[14]

In addition to the popular revelry of the season alluded to in *Mankind*, there are both serious and parodic references to the liturgy of pre-Lent and Lent.[15] Sister Mary Philippa Coogan has shown that Mercy's speeches draw on liturgical verses of Lenten services, beginning with Ash Wednesday.[16] She emphasizes the portrayal of Mercy as a priest and friar who would be expected to preach the necessity of penitence and annual confession at that time of year, concluding that "*Mankind* seems to have been written especially to encourage people to keep a good Lent."[17] I have also made the argument that the liturgy and homilies of the Sundays after Epiphany are the sources for a majority of the themes and biblical allusions in *Mankind*, whether those are preached by Mercy, used by Mankind as he attempts to fight off his tempters, or perverted in the nonsense babble of the Worldlings.[18] The major liturgical themes are the wisdom and power of God's word, which arm the soul for the battle against

---

[10] According to Sponsler, *Drama and Resistance*, p. 79.

[11] Bonnie Blackburn and Leofranc Holford-Strevens give a succinct summary of the complicated and fluid calendrical details of "pre-Lent" (*Oxford Companion to the Year*, pp. 602–08). See also Pettitt, "*Mankind*: An English *Fastnachtspiel*?" p. 192; on European dramatic traditions of Carnival, see Eisenbichler and Hüsken, *Carnival and the Carnivalesque*. On Shrovetide games that have persisted across the centuries, see Margaret Baker, *Folklore and Customs of Rural England*, pp. 98–108.

[12] Hans-Jürgen Diller argues that the *quête* in *Mankind* "reminds us of a *Heischegang*, a begging tour as it is known from popular customs around Christmas and Shrove Tuesday" ("Laughter in Medieval English Drama," p. 14). Such features of the season were especially associated with young men, which leads Diller to posit an audience of college students in the Cambridge vicinity for the play (p. 15).

[13] Pettitt, "*Mankind*: An English *Fastnachtspiel*?" p. 193.

[14] Axton, *European Drama*, p. 201. Neville Denny, "Aspects of the Staging of *Mankind*," argues even more emphatically and at greater length for the importance of Mummers' Play style and stage "business" in *Mankind*.

[15] Richard Axton says, "If it was *for* the folk the play was certainly not *by* the folk, and one is tempted to see it as the Shrovetide *jeu d'esprit* of a group of Cambridge clerks" (*European Drama*, p. 201).

[16] Coogan, *Interpretation of the Moral Play, Mankind*, pp. 10–56.

[17] Coogan, *Interpretation of the Moral Play, Mankind*, p. 55.

[18] Ashley, "Battle of Words."

evil — the temptations of foolish talk and the lies of the devil. Images of sowing seed also recur during this post-Epiphany season, with references to such parables as the sowing of weeds in a field of good seed (Matthew 13:24–30), the man who sows seed on various kinds of ground (Luke 8:4–15), and the parable of the vineyard (Matthew 20:1–16). These images were usually understood to refer to language as well as actions that would lead to salvation or damnation at the Judgment Day, as I have shown.[19]

*Mankind*, then, dramatizes a battle between Carnival and Lent, between festive revelry and sober penitence.[20] There is disagreement, however, about how successfully the Lenten sermons of Mercy might have weighed against the comic spectacle provided by the worldly and demonic characters of *Mankind*. Do the vices ultimately intensify or undermine the moral and doctrinal instruction? Some critics suggest that the vices are given such dramatic vitality that they upstage Mercy.[21] Anthony Gash sketches out the medieval antithesis of official ecclesiastical doctrine and popular festive culture, arguing that the play — usually treated as a morality — enacts a balance or "ambivalence." For Gash, "it is more usefully seen as compounding two genres, one official, the other unofficial, by punning between the morality play structure (the fall, repentance and salvation of mankind) and a festive structure (the battle between the licence of Christmas and the prohibitions of Lent)."[22] The vices, he suggests, "open up every form of equivocation which the closed formal discourse of Mercy seeks to seal off."[23] Michael T. Peterson goes even further, arguing that the presentation of a plurality of discourses within the play in effect undermines God's position as the supreme guarantor of meaning.[24]

SOCIAL PROTEST

The unruly and "grotesque body" on display in *Mankind* is also socially subversive, and we know that pre-Lenten winter festivities could occasionally provide an opportunity for political protest — as they did in the case of John Gladman, a Norwich guildsman dressed as the "King of Christmas," who in 1443 led a riotous procession (of a type identified as a Shrove Tuesday procession in the records) with other artisans and fellow citizens to manifest their unhappiness

---

[19] Ashley, "Battle of Words," pp. 136–38, especially notes 17–20.

[20] The theme of a battle between Carnival and Lent is also found in the visual arts, for example Peter Brueghel's famous painting of *The Fight between Carnival and Lent*; see color plates 3 and 4 in Stechow, *Pieter Bruegel the Elder*, pp. 56–59.

[21] See, for example, Watkins, "Allegorical Theatre," p. 77. In making his argument about the homoerotic context of male lechery in *Mankind*, Garrett Epp too notes that allegory is a "notoriously slippery medium, particularly in the theatre" ("Vicious Guise," p. 305); thus, while "effeminacy is personified in order to condemn it as vicious," the identity that is imposed on the characters, "threatening to turn them into a discourse of pure vice and virtue, is inhabited by an actual body that is not so easily defined or contained" (pp. 304–05).

[22] Gash, "Carnival against Lent," p. 82. As Gash points out, the term "Christmas" had a much less restricted sense than it does now, and could refer to the extended season of festivity that began in December and lasted until Shrove Tuesday (p. 83).

[23] Gash, "Carnival against Lent," p. 94.

[24] Peterson, *"Fragmina Verborum,"* p. 163.

at the policies of local monastic officials.[25] Mankind, the protagonist of our play, is portrayed not as an urban citizen but as a poor farmer in a rural setting; however, Gash calls attention to "a variety of doctrinal unorthodoxies and anti-clerical resentments which were probably an abiding facet of peasant and plebian attitudes."[26] Some of these, like Mankind's claim that he could skip church since prayer would sacralize his field (line 553) and transform it into a church-like space, were persecuted as Lollard heresy in fifteenth-century East Anglia.[27]

The figure of the rural laborer was a resonant one for late medieval culture.[28] The fourteenth-century alliterative narrative *Piers Plowman* uses the peasant as protagonist for its allegory, which combines both spiritual search and social critique.[29] John Ball, the country priest who led the 1381 peasant's uprising, famously preached political insurrection based on the proverbial couplet: "Whanne Adam dalfe and Eve span, / Who was thanne a gentil man?"[30] Within *Mankind*, the symbolism of working the earth operates at multiple interpretive levels. Typologically, Mankind has connections to Adam, whose original sin of disobedience to God was punished by a life of work, symbolized in medieval iconography by a spade.[31] Throughout the play, however, the spade takes on a positive moral valence as the symbol of the peasant's work ethic, the main defense he has against temptation.

The spade is Mankind's chief attribute from the time he first enters — presumably prop in hand — acknowledging man's creation by God, "Of the erth and of the cley we have owr propagacyon" (line 186). Mercy warns him about the dangers of temptation and urges him "Do truly yowr labure and kepe yowr halyday" (line 300). Still under the influence of Mercy's moral teachings, Mankind gets to work despite the pestering of New Guise, "Thys erth wyth my spade I shall assay to delffe" (line 328). He then uses it with comic efficacy to beat off the annoying distractions of the three Worldlings after a scene in which they mock his digging: "Go and do yowr labur! . . . / Or wyth my spade I shall yow dynge . . . / Have ye non other man to moke, but ever me?" (lines 376–78). As the vices cry over their wounds, Mankind acknowl-

---

[25] Gash, "Carnival against Lent," pp. 85–86. See also the historical analysis of competing contemporary reports of the Gladman incident by Chris Humphrey, *Politics of Carnival*, pp. 63–82. Humphrey argues that festive misrule is not "*intrinsically* political" but becomes so when its imagery is relevant to a local situation (p. 78).

[26] Gash, "Carnival against Lent," p. 95.

[27] On this Lollard tenet, see Forest-Hill, "*Mankind* and the Fifteenth-Century Preaching Controversy," p. 22.

[28] See Alexander, "*Labeur* and *Paresse*."

[29] For a survey of the "plebian voice" (especially that of agricultural labor) in the period after the peasant's rebellion of 1381, see Aers, "*Vox Populi* and the Literature of 1381." On *Piers Plowman's* relation to the 1381 uprising, see Justice, "*Piers Plowman* in the Rising," in his *Writing and Rebellion*, pp. 102–39.

[30] On the couplet, see Friedman, "'When Adam Delved.'"

[31] For images of Adam's spade, see Camille, "'When Adam Delved': Laboring on the Land." Clopper observes that while the image of Adam is certainly recalled in Mankind's labor, there is a significant difference in the depiction of Mankind's fall from that of Adam because of the comic portrayal of his adversaries: "But this is no Adam facing off the Arch-enemy of man; instead, we have a somewhat pompous farmer who is oblivious to the presence of his third-rate 'tempter' . . . The scene of Mankynd's fall best illustrates the play's ambience; it is a serious action treated comically without losing its significance" ("*Mankind* and Its Audience," p. 353).

edges with a biblical quote (1 Samuel 17:47) that his weapon was not a sword or spear, "Yyt this instrument, soverens, ys not made to defende. / Davide seyth, '*Nec in hasta nec in gladio salvat Dominus,*'" to which Nought responds with a parody of the Latin, "No, mary, I beschrew yow, yt ys in *spadibus*" (lines 396–98). Only when the devil Titivillus places a board under the soil, frustrating his digging, does Mankind finally discard the spade — that is, gives up a socially and spiritually virtuous activity — "Here I gyff uppe my spade for now and for ever" (line 549). A stage direction on the side calls attention to Mankind's defeat, symbolized by the cast-off spade: "Here Titivillus goth out wyth the spade" (after line 549).

While drawing on the various universalizing metaphors linking the spade with human labor, *Mankind* also calls attention to the economic realities underlying the misbehavior of marginal groups like the "disgruntled laborer" that Claire Sponsler identifies as troubling the "social imaginary of late medieval England."[32] As Mankind attempts to do his work, the vices remind him of the relative fruitlessness of his physical labor, with the implication that he will never make a living at it (lines 351–75). They may be reprehensible idlers, but their jokes articulate some of the complaints of agricultural laborers.[33] In addition, as Victor I. Scherb points out, the "thievery and murder urged by the Vices reflect local conditions in East Anglia during the 1450s and 1460s," when crime and violence were endemic to a region in economic crisis.[34]

Kellie Robertson terms the vices' "wandering ways" a kind of "camp criminality" that "highlights contemporary fears about vagrancy and non-work," arguing that rather than assuming a binary of work and idleness the play actually interrogates such categories.[35] She reads the play as "part of a larger response to anxieties about the spiritual and social regulation of 'true labor.'"

## LITERARY INTERPRETATIONS

Until the mid-1970s, *Mankind* was nearly universally condemned as being a corrupt and unsuccessful morality play.[36] Lorraine Kochanske Stock has assembled the verdicts of early critics; they include the accusations of plotlessness, structural imbalance by too many vice figures, and corruption of the serious morality by pointless humor, obscenity, and unnecessary

---

[32] Sponsler, *Drama and Resistance*, p. 82. See especially her discussion of the "Disgruntled Laborer," pp. 84–89, and the references cited in her notes 28, 29, 30, and 43 for the laws, attitudes, and representations of labor and peasants in late medieval Europe.

[33] For Victor I. Scherb, "Mankind is more than just a product of past texts . . . he was also a social reality — a fifteenth-century laborer, and the playwright exerts himself to bring that social reality before his audience" (*Staging Faith*, p. 119).

[34] Scherb, *Staging Faith*, pp. 124–26.

[35] Robertson, *Laborer's Two Bodies*, p. 168. Hers is the most in-depth analysis of Mankind's topical satire on the fifteenth-century problems with agricultural labor, which were addressed but also exacerbated by the 1446 statutes.

[36] Coogan's 1947 study was the lone exception in supporting the idea that *Mankind* demonstrated a careful three-part structure and intellectual design. See especially *Interpretation of the Moral Play, Mankind*, pp. 92–110.

horseplay.[37] The mid-1970s were pivotal in changing that early critical assessment, as multiple articles appeared that, although written independently, made the case for the thematic and structural unity of the play.

Stock calls attention to Mercy's recommendation of patience as an important virtue in the fight against temptation. She argues that the Instruction and Temptation scenes in *Mankind* contain verbal echoes of the Book of Job, beginning with Mankind's reference to his own flesh as "that stynkyng dungehyll" (line 204). Mercy asks Mankind to follow the example of Job, and Mankind does pin the text for Ash Wednesday (based on the Book of Job) to his chest to remind him of his mortality: *Memento, homo, quod cinis est, et in cinerem verteris*. Stock also asks us to see the three vices as parodies of Job's three friends, and finally chides critics who have "concentrated their energies on sanctimoniously denouncing the scatological elements in the play, devoting little attention, if any, to the eschatological concerns of *Mankind*."[38]

Paula Neuss pointed out that *Mankind*, adapting a strategy from medieval preaching, uses verbal images that are "repeated and interrelated in varying patterns" so that "something spoken becomes something seen."[39] For Neuss, the theme to which all images are related is that of "*Accedia*, or Sloth (as the *Castle of Perseverance* is concerned with Covetousness, or the *Pride of Life* with Pride)."[40] Neuss's article focuses in particular on the necessity to avoid such forms of Sloth as idle language and impatience, which lead to the fatal sin of despair. In the penultimate scene of the play, a desperate Mankind contemplates suicide, calling for a rope to hang himself after succumbing to temptation, because he is sure that he has forfeited mercy (line 800). Only Mercy's entrance to offer forgiveness — available up to the Last Judgment he reminds both the protagonist and the audience — rescues Mankind.

In a related argument, I have argued that the play is thematically and dramatically structured by a "battle of words" — where the "confrontation between good and evil is dramatized as a battle of good words ('predycacyon,' 'talking delectable,' 'few wordys,' and 'doctrine monytorye') against misleading or evil ones ('ydull language,' 'japyng,' 'many wordys,' and 'fablys delusory')."[41] The theme of language in the play is stylistically embodied in the diction and rhyme scheme employed by the different characters. Mercy, the preacher and father confessor to Mankind, uses an elevated style appropriate to his doctrinal message; it is a stately eight-line stanza rhyming *ababbcbc*, with polysyllabic words of Latin derivation. The four vices maintain a breathless stream of jokes, derision, and vulgarity, speaking in eight-line tail-rhyme stanzas, typically rhyming *aaabcccb*. Indeed, as Stanton B. Garner, Jr., comments, "words themselves acquire a near-physicality which renders them verbal equivalents of stage props."[42] He goes on to suggest that as the vice figures parody Mercy's preaching, "mimickry and rhyme deflect attention away from the meaning of words and onto their more strictly phonetic characteristics, while doggerel breaks the logic of

---

[37] Stock, "Thematic and Structural Unity of *Mankind*," pp. 386–87. For a recent discussion of the play's critical fortunes with an emphasis on what production can tell us, see also Brannen, "Century of *Mankind*."

[38] Stock, "Thematic and Structural Unity of *Mankind*," p. 407.

[39] Neuss, "Active and Idle Language," p. 44.

[40] Neuss, "Active and Idle Language," p. 44.

[41] Ashley, "Battle of Words," p. 130.

[42] Garner, "Theatricality in *Mankind* and *Everyman*," p. 278.

syntax on which comprehension depends, setting words loose in a non-referential free-for-all. . . . 'Misshe-masche, driff-draff.'"[43] Mankind's moral state is signaled by the style he adopts — the aureate style when following Mercy and pell-mell rhythms when swayed by the vices.[44]

The centrality of language to the play's action and message perhaps explains the choice of a devil (usually known as Tutivillus) to be the chief demonic agent of Mankind's sin. In sermons and treatises, Tutivillus was a minor devil charged with collecting verbal misdemeanors: syllables dropped by priests in saying mass, gossiping words exchanged by women in church, idle words, etc. Tutivillus was to put these offending words or parts of words into his sack — or write them on his scroll — and bring them to the Last Judgment. The Towneley cycle *Judgement* play, in fact, concludes with a long scene featuring the demon Tutivillus, who describes himself as the devil's registrar and now master lollard, collecting ill-spoken words ("fragmina verborum / tutivillus colligit horum") as he ushers the damned off to hell.[45] In *Mankind*, his name has been altered to Titivillus, and he plays the important role of the demonic trickster who succeeds in causing Mankind's fall into idleness and sin. With his lies he is the dramatic embodiment of verbal temptation.[46]

Recent criticism has explored *Mankind's* thematics of language by scrutinizing even more intensely Mercy's Latinate English as the controversial representation of fifteenth-century preaching. Janette Dillon focuses on the Worldlings' parody of Mercy's latinate discourse by using Latin themselves:

> Not only do they mock Mercy with Latinate English, translate obscenities into Latin and mingle Latin with English in a kind of macaronic carnival; they also make up pseudo-Latin words from English roots, utter mock prayers and blessings, . . . construct a prolonged pseudo-trial (suggesting the Last Judgment) in a mixture of English, Latin, and pseudo-Latin and play with the sheer sound of Latin until it is reduced to nonsense.[47]

The play dramatizes issues of ecclesiastical discourse that had been politicized in the Lollard and anti-Lollard rhetoric of the fifteenth century. The use of English rather than Latin by the clergy or writers was a hotly debated topic, and Dillon proposes that *Mankind* invites its audience to defamiliarize the "priestly dialect" that linked "Latinity and truth."[48] *Mankind*, she says, challenges the "excessive Latinity" of orthodox preaching, and thus suggests that

---

[43] Garner, "Theatricality in *Mankind* and *Everyman*," p. 278.

[44] Ashley, "Battle of Words," p. 131.

[45] *Towneley Plays*, ed. Pollard, p. 375, line 251. Margaret Jennings provides the fullest compendium of medieval references to this minor devil, "Tutivillus: The Literary Career of the Recording Demon." See also Neuss, "Active and Idle Language," pp. 55–64.

[46] On this topic, see Ashley, "Battle of Words," pp. 128–30. W. A. Davenport argues that the amplification of Titivillus into an important character in *Mankind* parallels the development of the minor demon Treselincellis into a more important spiritual threat in Peter Idley's mid-fifteenth-century *Instructions to His Son*, whether or not the treatise was an actual source for the play ("Peter Idley and the Devil in *Mankind*.").

[47] Dillon, "Politics of 'Englysch Laten,'" p. 57.

[48] Dillon, "Politics of 'Englysch Laten,'" p. 52.

Latin may be used to utter blasphemies just as plain English may be used to utter sacred truths.[49]

Lynn Forest-Hill, too, takes up the theme of language as it was used within the context of fifteenth-century East Anglian preaching manuals that addressed the threat of Lollardy. Forest-Hill argues that *Mankind* belongs to the large number of works of the century addressed either to Lollards or to the problems they posed to orthodoxy. The vernacular works of Reginald Pecock, for example, were examined for heresy, but he defended his orthodoxy and explained that he chose to write in English in order to "challenge the heretical opinions of the Lollards in the language they themselves favored."[50] The play echoes preaching manuals that condemn people who mock preachers, but also includes discussion of what makes preaching effective — namely, the intentions of both speaker and listener.[51] The mere uttering of words in Latin does not guarantee legitimacy; in the play, for example, Mankind writes and quotes biblical verse in Latin, but then falls to temptation, while the devil enters declaring "*Ego sum dominancium dominus,* and my name ys Titivillus" (line 475). The audience of *Mankind* was obviously expected to differentiate between a virtuous use of language and a vicious one — whether that language was Latin *or* English.

## ENGAGING THE AUDIENCE

Typically, the morality play addresses its edifying message as much to the audience as to the central character, and *Mankind* develops the technique with great sophistication. When Mercy makes his long aureate speeches of doctrinal and moral instruction at the beginning and the end of the play, he is alone on the stage addressing the audience: "O soverence, I beseche yow yowr condycyons to rectyfye / . . . I have be the very mene for yowr restytucyon. / Mercy ys my name, that mornyth for yowr offence. / Dyverte not yowrsylffe in tyme of temtacyon, / That thee may be acceptable to Gode at yowr goyng hence" (lines 13 and 17–20). He ends his forty-four-line speech again "beseeching" the audience to pay attention to his warning about the devices of the tempters, "I besech yow hertyly, have this premedytacyon" (line 44).[52] Our protagonist, Mankind, enters for the first time only at line 185 after Mercy has been taunted by the four vice figures, demonstrating the truth of Mercy's words and dramatizing the linguistic nature of the upcoming temptations. Likewise, at the end of the play, Mankind exits the stage after line 902, leaving Mercy to address the audience in a parallel speech to the opening: "Wyrschepyll sofereyns, I have do my propirté: / . . . / Serge your condicyons wyth dew examinacion. / Thynke and remembyr the world ys but a vanité, / . . . / Therefore God grant yow all *per suam misericordiam* / That ye may be pley-ferys wyth the angellys above / And have to your porcyon *vitam eternam. Amen!*" (lines 903, 908–09, and 912–14).

---

[49] Dillon, "Politics of 'Englysch Laten,'" p. 59.

[50] Forest-Hill, "*Mankind* and the Fifteenth-Century Preaching Controversy," p. 20.

[51] Forest-Hill, "*Mankind* and the Fifteenth-Century Preaching Controversy," p. 29.

[52] Liliana Sikorska argues that the dramatic effect of the entire play is dependent upon the use of such "highly rhetorical" directives which "have a non-literary illocutionary force, in the sense that their primary point of reference is the actual world, not the one represented in the play" ("*Mankind* and the Question of Power Dynamics," p. 214).

When New Guise, Nowadays, and Nought reach the height of their diverting activity, they invite the audience to join with them in singing an obscene "Crystemes songe" (line 332). As Pamela King notes, the result is that the audience succumbs to idleness of the tongue — a major sin the play preaches against — even before the protagonist.[53] Titivillus the devil, too, when he enters to seduce Mankind into sin, establishes a partnership with the audience, as Meg Twycross and Sarah Carpenter have argued.[54] The audience's desire for sensation had already been manipulated when the vices collected money with the promise of seeing the "man wyth a hede that ys of grett omnipotens" (line 461). Titivillus is invisible to Mankind, so it is the play's audience who can visually participate in the temptations the devil enacts. They become "accomplices in his plots and his joke against Mankind,"[55] and when Titivillus says, "I am here ageyn to make this felow yrke"(line 556), he is speaking to the audience. He then calls for their silence as he begins to whisper sinister thoughts into Mankind's ear as he sleeps: "Qwyst! Pesse! I shall go to hys ere and tytyll therin. / . . . / Ande ever ye dyde, for me kepe now yowr sylence" (lines 557 and 589). Through the scene, the audience itself is tricked into complicity with the devil's machinations against Mankind, a technique of addressing and implicating the audience that is present throughout the play, whether good or evil characters are on stage.

## THE EAST ANGLIAN CONTEXT

The intense and sustained engagement of this morality play with its audience is only strengthened by the dialogue's topical humor based on references to people and places they probably knew. *Mankind* is written in the East Midland dialect found in Cambridgeshire, Norfolk, and Suffolk. References in the play confirm its placement in Cambridgeshire; for example, the three vices New Guise, Nowadays, and Nought say they will find several men that W. K. Smart has identified as actual historical residents of the region in the late fifteenth century.[56] Place-names given in the dialogue between lines 505 and 515 confirm the East Anglian connection. These include Fulbourn, Bottisham, and Swaffham to the east of Cambridge, and Sauston, Hauxton, and Trumpington south of Cambridge. Norfolk place names are Walton, Gayton, Massingham, and another Swaffham. Bury St. Edmunds, Suffolk, is mentioned in line 274, which is significant because two of the early owners of the manuscript came from Bury: Reverend Cox Macro and Thomas Hyngham, a monk at the monastery there.[57]

Despite its many unique features, therefore, the play *Mankind* clearly belongs to "the most important regional theatrical tradition in late medieval England" — that of East Anglia.[58] As

---

[53] King, "Morality Plays," p. 250.

[54] Twycross and Carpenter, *Masks and Masking,* p. 251.

[55] Twycross and Carpenter, *Masks and Masking,* p. 251.

[56] Smart, "Some Notes on *Mankind*," pp. 48–55.

[57] On the importance of the monastery at Bury St. Edmunds for the history of the Macro manuscript and for East Anglian drama in general, see Gibson, *Theater of Devotion,* especially pp. 107–17. Gibson argues that the monks of the Benedictine monastery at Bury "helped create one of the most diverse and important English dramatic traditions of the fifteenth century" (p. 108).

[58] Coldewey, "Non-Cycle Plays and the East Anglian Tradition," pp. 189–210.

Victor I. Scherb notes, judging by the number of surviving texts alone, "East Anglia was the West End or Broadway of fifteenth- and early sixteenth-century England."[59]

## THE TEXT

*Mankind* survives in a unique fifteenth-century manuscript that also contains two other Middle English morality plays, the *Castle of Perseverance* and *Wisdom*. The Macro Manuscript (MS V.a. 354 in the Folger Library collection, Washington, DC) is a compilation of plays copied from separate sources, as well as unrelated pieces. Peter Happé argues that the Macro plays — with their mixture of Latin learning and staging references — appear to serve two purposes, both as devotional text and script for performance.[60] Clues to the dating of *Mankind* may be found within the text, most significantly the reference to a coin called the "royal," first minted in 1464–65. Moreover, the Worldlings in their joking patter refer to every late fifteenth-century English coin except the "angel." Since the angel was issued in 1468–70, it has been argued that the play was probably written between 1465 and 1470.[61]

The texts of *Mankind* and *Wisdom* were owned in the late fifteenth century by a monk named Hyngham, who names himself as owner on fols. 121v and 134r at the ends of *Wisdom* and *Mankind*, respectively. In the sixteenth century, Robert Oliver also put his marks on the two plays, claiming ownership on fol. 134v of *Mankind*. A later owner of these two plays and a third, the *Castle of Perseverance*, was the Reverend Cox Macro (1683–1767), from whom the manuscript — now containing the three morality plays and other nondramatic works — received its name. After Reverend Macro, the manuscript passed to a relative, John Patteson of Norwich, and in 1820 was sold to the Gurney family of Keswick Hall, Norfolk, who put the three morality plays into a separate volume. In 1936, the Folger Library bought this manuscript and, in 1971, the library rebound the Macro manuscript, including all the original pieces.[62]

The present edition is based on David Bevington's facsimile edition of *The Macro Plays* to which we compared other editions, especially the Early English Text Society edition of *The Macro Plays* by Mark Eccles. In the manuscript the play presents few major textual problems, but, as Eccles notes, the scribe who copied *Wisdom* then wrote most of *Mankind* "so hastily that more emendations are needed."[63] After this scribe produced most of the text of *Mankind* (fols. 122–132), another concluded the play (fols. 132v–143). Both scribes separate the speeches of different characters by a line across the page. The main textual challenge is that a single leaf,

---

[59] Scherb, *Staging Faith*, p. 21. On pp. 23–24, he lists the manuscripts surviving from Norfolk, Suffolk, Cambridgeshire, and Essex.

[60] Happé, "Macro Plays Revisited."

[61] Donald C. Baker, "Date of *Mankind*."

[62] Although the reassembled manuscript no longer follows the original numbering in an early hand — which puts *Wisdom* on pages 98–121, *Mankind* on pages 122–34, and *Castle of Perseverance* on pages 154–91 — critical editions of *Mankind* have retained these page numbers.

[63] Eccles, "Macro Plays," p. 29. Richard Beadle reviews the complex arguments among textual scholars over the hands found in *Wisdom* and *Mankind*, finally supporting the argument of Eccles that one scribe copied both *Wisdom* and most of *Mankind* ("Scribal Problem in the Macro Manuscript."). More recently, Beadle has argued that Hyngham is the scribe who copied the plays ("Monk Thomas Hyngham's Hand in the Macro MS").

the original second leaf of seventy to eighty lines, is missing from the play between fols. 122 and 123, the present lines 71–72.

In this edition we have followed METS guidelines in writing thorns and edths as *th* and yoghs as *g*, *gh*, *y*, or *s*. We have regularized by capitalizing proper names and adding modern punctuation (virtually no punctuation appears in the manuscript). Certain emendations follow modern spelling conventions, e.g.,"beseche" for "be seche." Others were made to retain line sense when a likely scribal error occurred, e.g., "butcher" for "botther." However, we have remained true to late Middle English habits by retaining different spellings for the same words, e.g., "ther" and "there"; "you" and "yow." When an incomplete or abbreviated word appears, we have expanded it with a form that is compatible with other lines in the play.

MANUSCRIPT

Indexed as item 3495 in Boffey and Edwards, eds., *New Index of Middle English Verse*:

•Washington, Folger Shakespeare Library 5031, fols. 14–37. [The Macro Manuscript]

 # MANKIND

**DRAMATIS PERSONAE:**
MERCY
MISCHIEF
NEW GYSE
NOUGHT
NOWADAYS
MANKYNDE
TITIVILLUS

[*Enter Mercy*]

MERCY The very fownder and begynner of owr fyrst creacyon
    Amonge us synfull wrechys He oweth to be magnyfyde,    *ought; glorified*
    That for owr dysobedyenc He hade non indygnacyon    *did not refuse*
    To sende Hys own son to be torn and crucyfyede.
5    Owr obsequyouse servyce to Hym shulde be aplyede,
    Where He was Lorde of all and made all thynge of nought,
    For the synfull synnere to hade hym revyvyde
    And for hys redempcyon sett Hys own son at nought.[1]

    Yt may be seyde and veryfyede, mankynde was dere bought.[2]
10    By the pytuose deth of Jhesu he hade hys remedye.    *piteous*
    He was purgyde of hys defawte that wrechydly hade wrought
    By Hys gloryus passyon, that blyssyde lavatorye.
    O soverence, I beseche yow yowr condycyons to rectyfye[3]
    Ande wyth humylité and reverence to have a remocyon    *return*

---

[1] Lines 5–8: *Our dutiful service to Him [God] should be given, / Where He [who] was Lord of all and created all things from nothing, / On behalf of the sinful sinner in order to revive him / Sacrificed [set at nought] His own son for his [the sinner's] redemption*

[2] *It may be said and verified [that] mankind was dearly bought (ransomed)*

[3] Lines 11–13: *He who has sinned grievously was purged of his original sin / By His [Christ's] glorious suffering, that blessed purifier. / Oh worthy masters (audience members), I implore you to rectify your habits*

15  To this blyssyde prynce that owr nature doth gloryfye,
   That ye may be partycypable of Hys retribucyon.[1]

   I have be the very mene for yowr restytucyon.      *been the true means*
   Mercy ys my name, that mornyth for yowr offence.      *mourns*
   Dyverte not yowrsylffe in tyme of temtacyon,
20  That thee may be acceptable to Gode at yowr goyng hence.   *at your time of death*
   The grett mercy of Gode, that ys of most preemmynence,
   Be medyacyon of Owr Lady that ys ever habundante   *By intercession; bountiful*
   To the synfull creature that wyll repent hys neclygence,   *sinfulness*
   I prey Gode, at yowr most nede, that mercy be yowr defendawnte.

25  In goode werkys I avyse yow, soverence, to be perseverante   *advise you, masters*
   To puryfye yowr sowlys, that thei be not corupte;     *so that*
   For yowr gostly enmy wyll make hys avaunte,
   Yowr goode condycyons yf he may interrupte.[2]

   O ye soverens that sytt and ye brothern that stonde ryght uppe,   *you noble persons*
30  Pryke not yowr felycytes in thyngys transytorye.     *Place; happiness*
   Beholde not the erth, but lyfte yowr ey uppe.      *eye*
   Se how the hede the members dayly do magnyfye.     *head; worship*
   Who ys the hede forsoth I shall yow certyfye:
   I mene Owr Savyowr, that was lykynnyde to a lambe;    *likened*
35  Ande Hys sayntys be the members that dayly He doth satysfye  *by the parts of the body*
   Wyth the precyose rever that runnyth from Hys wombe.[3]   *river*

   Ther ys non such foode, be water nor by londe,
   So precyouse, so gloryouse, so nedefull to owr entent,    *purpose*
   For yt hath dyssolvyde mankynde from the bytter bonde
40  Of the mortall enmye, that vemynousse serpente,
   From the wyche Gode preserve yow all at the Last Jugement!  *From whom*
   For sekyrly ther shall be a streyt examynacyon,     *surely; strict*
   The corn shall be savyde, the chaffe shall be brente.    *grain; burnt*
   I besech yow hertyly, have this premedytacyon.   *keep this thought in mind*

    *[Enter Mischief]*

**MISCHIEF** I beseche yow hertyly, leve yowr calcacyon.   *threshing (see note)*
46  Leve yowr chaffe, leve yowr corn, leve yowr dalyacyon.   *idle chatter*
   Yowr wytt ys lytyll, yowr hede ys mekyll, ye are full of predycacyon.  *big; preaching*
   But, ser, I prey this questyon to claryfye:

---

[1] *That you may be able to participate in His reward*

[2] Lines 27–28: *For your spiritual enemy (the devil) will make his boast, / If he can interrupt your good (spiritual) habits*

[3] *Life-giving blood (precious river) poured out from the crucified Christ's womb-like side*

Mysse-masche, dryff-draff,
50 Sume was corn and sume was chaffe, *wheat*
My dame seyde my name was Raffe;
Onschett yowr lokke and take an halpenye. *Open your "purse"; halfpenny [for me]*

**MERCY** Why com ye hethyr, brother? Ye were not dysyryde. *welcome (desired)*
**MISCHIEF** For a wynter corn-threscher, ser, I have hyryde, *Because*
55 Ande ye sayde the corn shulde be savyde and the chaff shulde be feryde, *burnt (fired)*
And he provyth nay, as yt schewth be this verse: *But; is shown by*
"*Corn servit bredibus, chaffe horsibus, straw fyrybusque.*"[1]
Thys ys as moche to say, to yowr leude undyrstondynge, *unlearned*
As the corn shall serve to brede at the nexte bakynge.

60 "*Chaff horsybus et reliqua,*" *and the rest*
The chaff to horse shall be goode provente, *provender*
When a man ys forcolde the straw may be brent, *very cold*
And so forth, et cetera.

**MERCY** Avoyde, goode brother! Ye ben culpable *Go away*
65 To interrupte thus my talkyng delectable.
**MISCHIEF** Ser, I have nother horse nor sadyll, *neither*
Therfor I may not ryde.
**MERCY** Hye yow forth on fote, brother, in Godys name! *Hurry*
**MISCHIEF** I say, ser, I am cumme hedyr to make yow game. *come hither to have fun with you*
70 Yet bade ye me not go out in the devyllys name,
Ande I wyll abyde.

**MERCY** . . .

[A page is missing from the manuscript. It seems that Mischief continues to pester Mercy and then departs. New Guise, Nowadays, and Nought enter; the former two attempt to make Nought join in their foolhardy and very physical games and dances, but he will not. As the action resumes below they are flogging Nought's belly — perhaps tickling him — until it will "burst." When they have exhausted Nought, they force Mercy into the "dance."]

**NEW GYSE** Ande how, mynstrellys, pley the comyn trace! *popular dance*
73 Ley on wyth thi ballys tyll hys bely breste! *bales (whips)*
**NOUGHT** I putt case I breke my neke: how than? *suppose; will break; what*
**NEW GYSE** I gyff no force, by Sent Tanne! *I care not; Saint Anne*
**NOWADAYS** Leppe about lyvely! Thou art a wyght man. *Leap; nimble*
Lett us be mery wyll we be here! *while*
**NOUGHT** Shall I breke my neke to schew yow sporte?
**NOWADAYS** Therfor ever beware of thi reporte. *In that case; talk*

---

[1] *Wheat serves for bread, chaff for horses, and straw for fires (nonsense Latin)*

**NOUGHT**  I beschrew ye all! Her ys a schrewde sorte.                    *curse; rascally*
81      Have theratt then wyth a mery chere!                                    *Take this*

*Her thei daunce. Mercy seyth:*

**MERCY**  Do wey, do wey this reull, sers! Do wey!                         *Stop; revelry*
**NOWADAYS**  Do wey, goode Adam? Do wey?
        Thys ys no parte of thi pley.                                           *concern*
**NOUGHT**  Yys, mary, I prey yow, for I love not this revelynge.      *surely (or "By Mary")*
86      Cum forth, goode fader, I yow prey!                                    *(i.e., Mercy)*
        Be a lytyll ye may assay.                                      *With a little effort; try*

        Anon, of your wyth yowr clothes, yf ye wyll play.[1]
89      Go to! For I have hade a praty scottlynge.                          *pretty caper*

*[They try to get Mercy to dance]*

**MERCY**  Nay, brother, I wyll not daunce.
**NEW GYSE**  Yf ye wyll, ser, my brother wyll make yow to prawnce.
**NOWADAYS**  Wyth all my herte, ser, yf I may yow avaunce.                        *aid*
        Ye may assay be a lytyll trace.                                  *try (it); dance*
**NOUGHT**  Ye, ser, wyll ye do well                                          *[ironic]*
95      Trace not wyth them, be my cownsell,                                  *Dance*
        For I have tracyed sumwhat to fell;                      *danced; too violently*
        I tell yt ys a narow space.                                        *crowded*

        But, ser, I trow of us thre I herde yow speke.                    *believe*
**NEW GYSE**  Crystys curse hade therfor, for I was in slepe.              *[I] had*
**NOWADAYS** And I hade the cuppe in my honde, redy to goo to met.  *supper (solid food)*
101     Therfor, ser, curtly, grett yow well.                          *quickly, greet*
**MERCY**  Few wordys, few and well sett!                              *(i.e., I'll be brief)*
**NEW GYSE**  Ser, yt ys the new gyse and the new jett.                  *style; custom*
        Many wordys and shortely sett,
105     Thys ys the new gyse, every-dele.                                 *every bit*

**MERCY**  Lady, helpe! How wrechys delyte in ther synfull weys!      *Our Lady (Mary)*
**NOWADAYS**  Say not ageyn the new gyse nowadays!                          *against*
        Thou shall fynde us schrewys at all assays.          *rascals in every circumstance*
109     Beware! Ye may son lyke a boffett.                        *soon get (taste) a blow*
**MERCY**  He was well occupyede that browte yow brethern.[2]
**NOUGHT**  I harde yow call "New Gyse, Nowadays, Nought," all thes thre togethere.   *heard*
        Yf ye sey that I lye, I shall make yow to slyther.            *crawl on the ground*
113     Lo, take yow here a trepett!                                          *trip*

---

[1] *Quickly, off with your clothes (i.e., priest's vestments) if you wish to play*

[2] *He who brought you here was [and you are] wasting his [and your] time [ironic]*

[*They trip Mercy*]

**MERCY** Say me yowr namys, I know yow not.               *Tell*
**NEW GYSE** New Gyse, I.
**NOWADAYS**         I, Nowadays.
**NOUGHT**                I, Nought.
**MERCY** Be Jhesu Cryst that me dere bowte[1]
    Ye betray many men.
**NEW GYSE** Betray? Nay, nay, ser, nay, nay!         *sir*
    We make them both fresch and gay.
120     But of yowr name, ser, I yow prey,
    That we may yow ken.               *know*

**MERCY** Mercy ys my name by denomynacyon.     *designation*
    I conseyve ye have but a lytyll favour in my communycacyon.   *comfort*
**NEW GYSE** Ey, ey! Yowr body ys full of Englysch Laten.
125     I am aferde yt wyll brest.         *afraid; burst*
    "*Pravo te,*" quod the bocher onto me     *I curse you; butcher*
    When I stale a leg of motun.        *stole; mutton*
    Ye are a stronge cunnyng clerke.     *very learned scholar*
**NOWADAYS** I prey yow hertyly, worschyppull clerke,
130     To have this Englysch mad in Laten:     *translated into*

    "I have etun a dyschfull of curdys,     *eaten; curds*
    Ande I have schetun yowr mowth full of turdys."   *shitten; turds*
    Now opyn yowr sachell wyth Laten wordys
    Ande sey me this in clerycall manere!     *clerkly (learned)*
135     Also I have a wyf, her name ys Rachell;
    Betuyx her and me was a gret batell;     *Between*
    Ande fayn of yow I wolde here tell     *gladly from; wish*
    Who was the most master.

**NOUGHT** Thy wyf Rachell, I dare ley twenti lyse.     *wager; lice*
**NOWADAYS** Who spake to thee, foll? Thou art not wyse!     *fool*
141     Go and do that longyth to thin offyce:   *what belongs to; duty*
    *Osculare fundamentum!*     *Kiss my ass*
**NOUGHT** [*to Mercy*] Lo, master, lo, here ys a pardon bely-mett.   *sufficient*
    Yt ys grawntyde of Pope Pokett,     *granted by*
145     Yf ye wyll putt yowr nose in hys wyffys sockett,   *vagina*
    Ye shall have forty days of pardon.

**MERCY** Thys ydyll language ye shall repent.
    Out of this place I wolde ye went.     *I wish you would go*
**NEW GYSE** Goo we hens all thre wyth on assent.     *one accord*

---

[1] *By Jesus Christ who dearly (at a great cost) redeemed me*

150     My fadyr ys yrke of owr eloquence.                    *father (i.e., priest) is bothered by*
        Therfor I wyll no lenger tary.                                              *remain*
        Gode brynge yow, master and blyssyde Mary
        To the number of the demonycall frayry!              *brotherhood of demonic friars*

**NOWADAYS**   Cum wynde, cum reyn,
155     Thow I cumme never ageyn!                                  *I'll never come back*
        The Devll put out both yowr eyn!                                        *eyes*
        Felouse, go we hens tyght.                          *Fellows; quickly (together)*
**NOUGHT**   Go we hens, a devll wey!                           *the way of the devil*
        Here ys the dore, her ys the wey.
160     Farwell, jentyll Jaffrey,                          *gentle Geoffrey (i.e., Mercy)*
        I prey Gode gyf yow now goode nyght!

        *Exiant simul. Cantent.*                     *Let them go out together. They sing*

**MERCY**   Thankyde be Gode, we have a fayer dylyverance             *good riddance*
        Of thes thre onthryfty gestys.                              *unthrifty guests*
        They know full lytyll what ys ther ordynance.               *appointed place*
165     I preve by reson thei be wers then bestys:                          *beasts*

        A best doth after hys naturall instytucyon;                          *beast*
        Ye may conseyve be there dysporte and behavour,                         *by*
        Ther joy ande delyte ys in derysyon
        Of her owyn Cryste to hys dyshonur.

170     Thys condycyon of levyng, yt ys prejudycyall;
        Beware therof, yt ys wers than ony felony or treson.
        How may yt be excusyde befor the Justyce of all
        When for every ydyll worde we must yelde a reson?

        They have grett ease, therfor thei wyll take no thought.         *pay no mind*
175     But how then when the angell of hevyn shall blow the trumpe  *(i.e., But how they will)*
        And sey to the transgressors that wykkydly hath wrought,          *committed sin*
        "Cum forth onto yowr Juge and yelde yowr acownte?"

        Then shall I, Mercy, begyn sore to wepe;                           *bitterly*
        Nother comfort nor cownsell ther shall non be hade;                *Neither*
180     But such as thei have sowyn, such shall thei repe.                 *sown; reap*
        Thei be wanton now, but then shall thei be sade.

        The goode new gyse nowadays I wyll not dysalow.                      *forbid*
        I dyscomende the vycyouse gyse; I prey have me excusyde,[1]

---

[1] *I disapprove of the vicious behavior; I beg you, excuse me*

I nede not to speke of yt, yowr reson wyll tell yt yow.
185    Take that ys to be takyn and leve that ys to be refusyde.

[*Enter Mankind, dressed as a laborer, with a spade*]

**MANKYNDE**   Of the erth and of the cley we have owr propagacyon.
        By the provydens of Gode thus be we deryvatt,                                    *derived*
        To whos mercy I recomende this holl congrygacyon:
        I hope onto hys blysse ye be all predestynatt.                             *destined (for grace)*

190    Every man for hys degré I trust shall be partycypatt,        *in his own fashion; a participant*
        Yf we wyll mortyfye owr carnall condycyon
        Ande owr voluntarye dysyres, that ever be pervercyonatt,                          *perverse*
        To renunce them and yelde us under Godys provycyon.                    *place ourselves; care*

        My name ys Mankynde. I have my composycyon
195    Of a body and of a soull, of condycyon contrarye.
        Betwyx them tweyn ys a grett dyvisyon;                                               *two*
        He that shulde be subjecte, now he hath the victory.[1]

        Thys ys to me a lamentable story
        To se my flesch of my soull to have governance.
200    Wher the goodewyff ys master, the goodeman may be sory.                       *wife; husband*
        I may both syth and sobbe, this ys a pytouse remembrance.                      *sigh; piteous*

        O thou my soull, so sotyll in thy substance,                                   *delicate*
        Alasse, what was thi fortune and thi chaunce
        To be assocyat wyth my flesch, that stynkyng dungehyll?

205    Lady, helpe! Soverens, yt doth my soull myche yll                         *Our Lady (Mary)*
        To se the flesch prosperouse and the soull trodyn under fote.
        I shall go to yondyr man and asay hym y wyll.                                  *appeal to*
        I trust of gostly solace he wyll be my bote.                              *spiritual; helper*

        All heyll, semely father! Ye be welcom to this house.                       *well-dresssed*
210    Of the very wysdam ye have partycypacyon.                                          *true*
        My body wyth my soule ys ever querulose.                                        *at war*
        I prey yow, for sent charyté, of yowr supportacyon.

        I beseche yow hertyly of yowr gostly comforte.                        *spiritual guidance*
        I am onstedfast in lyvynge; my name ys Mankynde.
215    My gostly enmy the Devll wyll have a grett dysporte                              *sport*
        In synfull gydynge yf he may se me ende.[2]

---

[1] *He (i.e., the body) that should be the subject now has the victory (i.e., over the soul)*

[2] *So that he may see me end in sinful conduct*

| | | |
|---|---|---|
| **MERCY** | Cryst sende yow goode comforte! Ye be welcum, my frende. | |
| | Stonde uppe on yowr fete, I prey yow aryse. | |
| | My name ys Mercy; ye be to me full hende. | *welcome* |
| 220 | To eschew vyce I wyll yow avyse. | |

| | | |
|---|---|---|
| **MANKYNDE** | O Mercy, of all grace and vertu ye are the well, | *fountain* |
| | I have herde tell of ryght worschyppfull clerkys. | *from* |
| | Ye be aproxymatt to Gode and nere of hys consell. | *close* |
| | He hat instytut you above all hys werkys. | |

| | | |
|---|---|---|
| 225 | O, yowr lovely wordys to my soull are swetere then hony. | |
| **MERCY** | The temptacyon of the flesch ye must resyst lyke a man, | |
| | For ther ys ever a batell betwyx the soull and the body: | |
| | "*Vita hominis est milicia super terram.*"[1] | |

| | | |
|---|---|---|
| | Oppresse yowr gostly enmy and be Crystys own knyght. | |
| 230 | Be never a cowarde ageyn yowr adversary. | |
| | Yf ye wyll be crownyde, ye must nedys fyght. | |
| | Intende well and Gode wyll be yow adjutory. | *helper* |

| | | |
|---|---|---|
| | Remember, my frende, the tyme of contynuance. | *duration of life* |
| | So helpe me Gode, yt ys but a chery tyme. | *cherry time (see note)* |
| 235 | Spende yt well; serve Gode wyth hertys affyance. | *loyalty* |
| | Dystempure not yowr brayn wyth goode ale nor wyth wyn. | |

| | | |
|---|---|---|
| | Mesure ys tresure. Y forbyde yow not the use.[2] | |
| | Mesure yowrself ever; beware of excesse. | *Moderate* |
| | The superfluouse gyse I wyll that ye refuse; | *superfluous mode; wish* |
| 240 | When nature ys suffysyde, anon that ye sese. | *satisfied, then you [should] stop* |

| | | |
|---|---|---|
| | Yf a man have an hors and kepe hym not to hye, | *too well-fed* |
| | He may then reull hym at hys own dysyere. | *rule* |
| | Yf he be fede overwell he wyll dysobey | |
| | Ande in happe cast hys master in the myre. | *by chance; mire* |

[*Enter New Guise, Nowadays, and Nought, hidden to Mercy and Mankind*]

| | | |
|---|---|---|
| **NEW GYSE** | Ye sey trew, ser, ye are no faytour. | *liar* |
| 246 | I have fede my wyff so well tyll sche ys my master. | |
| | I have a grett wonde on my hede, lo! And theron leyth a playster, | *wound; plaster* |
| | Ande another ther I pysse my peson. | *where; penis (see note)* |
| | Ande my wyf were yowr hors, sche wold yow all to-banne. | *If; fully curse* |
| 250 | Ye fede yowr hors in mesure, ye are a wyse man. | *moderation (sarcastically)* |

---

[1] *The life of man upon earth is a warfare, [and his days are like the days of a hireling]* (Job 7:1)

[2] *Moderation is valuable. I do not forbid you to use ale or wine*

I trow, and ye were the kyngys palfrey-man,                    *believe, if; horsekeeper*
A goode horse shulde be gesunne.                                            *scarce*

**MANKYNDE**  [*hearing New Guise*] Wher spekys this felow? Wyll he not com nere?
**MERCY** All to son, my brother, I fere me, for yow.          *too soon (i.e., he will come)*
255    He was here ryght now, by Hym that bowte me dere,              *paid dearly for me*
        Wyth other of hys felouse; thei kan moche sorow.                *fellows; know*

        They wyll be here ryght son, yf I owt departe.              *very soon; go hence*
        Thynke on my doctryne; yt shall be yowr defence.
        Lerne wyll I am here; sett my wordys in herte.                       *while*
260    Wythin a schorte space I must nedys hens.                   *Soon I must depart*

**NOWADAYS**  [*unseen, to Mercy*] The sonner the lever, and yt be ewyn anon![1]
        I trow yowr name ys Do Lytyll, ye be so long fro hom.        *believe; far from*
        If ye wolde go hens, we shall cum everychon,                       *everyone*
        Mo then a goode sorte.                                    *More than a great many*
265    Ye have leve, I dare well say.                                    *permission*
        When ye wyll, go forth yowr wey.                                       *wish*
        Men have lytyll deynté of yowr pley                             *delight in*
        Because ye make no sporte.

**NOUGHT**  [*still unseen*] Yowr potage shall be forcolde, ser; when wyll ye go dyn?[2]
270    I have sen a man lost twenti noblys in as lytyll tyme;        *nobles (gold coins)*
        Yet yt was not I, be Sent Qwyntyn,                            *Saint Quentin*
        For I was never worth a pottfull a wortys sythyn I was born.  *cabbages since*
        My name ys Nought. I love well to make mery.
        I have be sethen wyth the comyn tapster of Bury              *just now; barkeeper*
275    And pleyde so longe the foll that I am evyn wery.             *fool; very weary*
        Yyt shall I be ther ageyn to-morn.                        *Yet; tomorrow morning*

**MERCY** I have moche care for yow, my own frende.          *concern; friend (i.e., Mankind)*
        Yowr enmys wyll be here anon, thei make ther avaunte.              *boast*
        Thynke well in yowr hert, yowr name ys Mankynde;
280    Be not unkynde to Gode, I prey yow be Hys servante.

        Be stedefast in condycyon; se ye be not varyant.              *easily changed*
        Lose not thorow foly that ys bowte so dere.          *through; bought so expensively*
        Gode wyll prove yow son; ande yf that ye be constant,                *test*
        Of Hys blysse perpetuall ye shall be partener.

285    Ye may not have yowr intent at yowr fyrst dysyere.                  *desire*
        Se the grett pacyence of Job in tribulacyon;

---

[1] *The sooner the better, and may it be right away*

[2] *Your soup shall be quite cold, sir; when will you dine*

Lyke as the smyth trieth ern in the feere,                          *blacksmith refines iron; fire*
So was he triede by Godys vysytacyon.                               *visitation (i.e., of trials)*

He was of yowr nature and of yowr fragylyté;                                      *He (i.e., Job)*
290  Folow the steppys of hym, my own swete sone,
Ande sey as he seyde in yowr trobyll and adversyté:
"*Dominus dedit, Dominus abstulit; sicut sibi placuit, sit nomen Domini benedictum!*"[1]

Moreover, in specyall I gyve yow in charge,                             *I advise you especially*
Beware of New Gyse, Nowadays, and Nought.
295  Nyse in ther aray, in language thei be large;                       *Foolish; dress; boastful*
To perverte yowr condycyons all the menys shall be sowte.               *habits; means; sought*

Gode son, intromytt not yowrsylff in ther cumpeny.[2]
Thei harde not a masse this twelmonyth, I dare well say.        *heard; year (twelve months)*
Gyff them non audyence; thei wyll tell yow many a lye.
300  Do truly yowr labure and kepe yowr halyday.                                      *holy day*

Beware of Tytivillus, for he lesyth no wey,                                      *he never fails*
That goth invysybull and wyll not be sen.                                      *Who goes; seen*
He wyll ronde in yowre ere and cast a nett befor yowr ey.                            *whisper*
He ys worst of them all; Gode lett hym never then!                         *never let him thrive*

305  Yf ye dysples Gode, aske mercy anon,                                *displease; immediately*
Ellys Myscheff wyll be redy to brace yow in hys brydyll.                  *Else; fasten; bridle*
Kysse me now, my dere darlynge. Gode schelde yow from yowr fon!                         *foes*
Do truly yowr labure and be never ydyll.
309  The blyssynge of Gode be wyth yow and wyth all thes worschyppull men!

     [*Exit*]

**MANKYNDE**   Amen, for sent charyté, amen!                                             *saint*

Now blyssyde be Jhesu! My soull ys well sacyatt                                      *satisfied*
Wyth the mellyfluose doctryne of this worschyppfull man.                *mellifluous; honorable*
The rebellyn of my flesch now yt ys superatt,                                        *overcome*
Thankynge be Gode of the commynge that I kam.                                  *that I came here*

315  Her wyll I sytt and tytyll in this papyr                                         *write on*
The incomparable astat of my promycyon.                                  *state; promised grace*
Worschypfull soverence, I have wretyn here
The gloryuse remembrance of my nobyll condycyon.

---

[1] *The Lord gave, and the Lord hath taken away: as it hath pleased the Lord so is it done: blessed be the name of the Lord* (Job 1:21)

[2] *Good son, don't put yourself in their company (i.e., don't hang around with them)*

To have remors and memory of mysylff thus wretyn yt ys,                    *In order that I may*
320    To defende me from all superstycyus charmys:
       "*Memento, homo, quod cinis es, et in cinerem reverteris.*"[1]

       [*Pointing to his breast, which bears this motto and perhaps a cross or a skull*]

       Lo, I ber on my bryst the bagge of myn armys.                       *breast; badge; arms*

       [*New Guise approaches Mankind*]

**NEW GYSE**   The wether ys colde, Gode sende us goode ferys!             *fires*
       "*Cum sancto sanctus eris et cum perverso perverteris.*"[2]
325    "*Ecce quam bonum et quam jocundum,*" quod the Devll to the frerys,
       "*Habitare fratres in unum.*"[3]

       [*Mankind picks up his spade and begins to till*]

**MANKYNDE**   I her a felow speke; wyth hym I wyll not mell.              *hear; associate*
       Thys erth wyth my spade I shall assay to delffe.                    *attempt to dig*
       To eschew ydullnes, I do yt myn own selffe.
330    I prey Gode sende yt hys fusyon!

       [*They approach Mankind*]

**NOWADAYS**   Make rom, sers, for we have be longe!                       *room; sirs; long (about)*
       We wyll cum gyf yow a Crystemes songe.                              *popular song (see note)*
**NOUGHT**   Now I prey all the yemandry that ys here                      *yeomanry (i.e., people)*
       To synge wyth us wyth a mery chere:

       [*They sing, leading the audience in the ditty*]

335    Yt ys wretyn wyth a coll, yt ys wretyn wyth a cole,                 *written; piece of coal*
**NEW GYSE AND NOWADAYS**   Yt ys wretyn wyth a colle, yt ys wretyn wyth a colle,
**NOUGHT**   He that schytyth wyth hys hoyll, he that schytyth wyth hys hoyll,   *shits; hole*
**NEW GYSE, NOWADAYS**   He that schytyth wyth hys hoyll, he that schytyth wyth hys hoyll,
**NOUGHT**   But he wyppe hys ars clen, but he wyppe hys ars clen,         *Unless; arse clean*
**NEW GYSE, NOWADAYS**   But he wype hys ars clen, but he wype hys ars clen,
**NOUGHT**   On hys breche yt shall be sen, on hys breche yt shall be sen,   *breeches; seen*

---

[1] *Remember, man, that you are dust, and unto dust you will return.* Similar to Job 34:15 and Genesis 3:19.

[2] "*With the holy, thou wilt be holy[; and with the innocent man thou wilt be innocent. And with the elect thou wilt be elect:] and with the perverse thou wilt be perverted*" (Psalm 17:26–27)

[3] Lines 325–26: "*Behold how good and how pleasant it is,*" said the Devil to the friars, / "*For brethren to dwell in unity*" (Psalm 132:1)

**NEW GYSE, NOWADAYS**  On hys breche yt shall be sen, on hys breche yt shall be sen.
*Cantant Omnes.* Hoylyke, holyke, holyke! Holyke, holyke, holyke!     *They all sing; holy (see note)*

**NEW GYSE**  Ey, Mankynde, Gode spede yow wyth yowr spade!
345     I shall tell yow of a maryage:
           I wolde yowr mowth and hys ars that this made                  *wish; i.e., composed this song*
           Wer maryede junctly together.                                          *married jointly*
**MANKYNDE**  Hey yow hens, felouse, wyth bredynge.                   *Hurry; from here; reproach*
           Leve yowr derysyon and yowr japyng.                                    *foolish talk*
350     I must nedys labure, yt ys my lyvynge.
**NOWADAYS**  What, ser, we cam but lat hethyr.                                 *recently here*

           Shall all this corn grow here                *Is this all [the space you have] here to grow grain*
           That ye shall have the nexte yer?                        *So that; have [grain for]*
           Yf yt be so, corn hade nede be dere,                      *better bring a good price*
355     Ellys ye shall have a pore lyffe.
**NOUGHT**  Alasse, goode fadere, this labor fretyth yow to the bon.          *wears you down*
           But for yowr croppe I take grett mone.                          *feel great sorrow*
           Ye shall never spende yt alonne;                                       *complete*
           I shall assay to geett yow a wyffe.                                         *try*

360     How many acres suppose ye here by estymacyon?
**NEW GYSE**  Ey, how ye turne the erth uppe and down!
           I have be in my days in many goode town
           Yett saw I never such another tyllynge.                        *Yet; such a tilling*

**MANKYNDE**  Why stonde ye ydyll? Yt ys pety that ye were born!                  *a pity*
**NOWADAYS**  We shall bargen wyth yow and nother moke nor scorne.             *neither*
366     Take a goode carte in hervest and lode yt wyth yowr corne,               *harvest*
           And what shall we gyf yow for the levynge?                             *crop*

**NOUGHT**  He ys a goode starke laburrer, he wolde fayn do well.             *strong; surely*
           He hath mett wyth the goode man Mercy in a schroude sell.          *at a bad time*
370     For all this he may have many a hungry mele.                 *Because of; meager meal*
           Yyt woll ye se he ys polytyke.[1]
           Here shall be goode corn, he may not mysse yt;
           Yf he wyll have reyn he may overpysse yt;                    *wishes to; piss on it*
           Ande yf he wyll have compasse he may overblysse yt          *compost; overbless it*
375     A lytyll wyth hys ars lyke.[2]                                            *arse*

**MANKYNDE**  Go and do yowr labur! Gode lett yow never the!                  *prosper*
           Or wyth my spade I shall yow dynge, by the Holy Trinyté!             *strike*
           Have ye non other man to moke, but ever me?                      *mock; always*

---

[1] *Yet you will see that he is prudent (i.e., despite Mercy's bad advice the crop will be good)*

[2] *Lines 374–75: I.e., in a blasphemous way, he may bless his crop with his feces*

Ye wolde have me of yowr sett?                                    *of your gang*
380    Hye yow forth lyvely, for hens I wyll yow dryffe.          *Hasten; hence; drive*

        [*Strikes them with his spade*]

**NEW GYSE**  Alas, my jewellys! I shall be schent of my wyff!    *testicles; rejected by (of no use to)*
**NOWADAYS**  Alasse! And I am lyke never for to thryve,
        I have such a buffett.                                   *injury [from being hit]*

**MANKYNDE**  Hens I sey, New Gyse, Nowadays, and Nowte!          *Go away*
385    Yt was seyde beforn, all the menys shuld be sought         *before; means*
        To perverte my condycyons and brynge me to nought.        *habits*
        Hens, thevys! Ye have made many a lesynge.               *Hence, thieves; lie*
**NOUGHT**  Marryde I was for colde, but now am I warme.          *Ruined; on account of*
        Ye are evyll avysyde, ser, for ye have don harme.         *ill-advised*
390    By cokkys body sakyrde, I have such a peyn in my arme      *Christ's sacred body*
        I may not chonge a man a ferthynge.[1]                   *change; farthing*

**MANKYNDE**  Now I thanke Gode, knelynge on my kne.
        Blyssyde be Hys name! He ys of hye degré.                *high estate*
        By the subsyde of Hys grace that He hath sente me         *help*
395    Thre of myn enmys I have putt to flyght.
        Yyt this instrument, soverens, ys not made to defende.
        Davide seyth, "*Nec in hasta nec in gladio salvat Dominus.*"[2]
**NOUGHT**  No, mary, I beschrew yow, yt ys in *spadibus.*        *curse you; by the spade*
        Therfor Crystys curse cum on yowr hedybus                 *head*
400    To sende yow lesse myght!

        *Exiant* [*except Mankind*]                              *They exit*

**MANKYNDE**  I promytt yow thes felouse wyll no more cum here,   *promise*
        For summe of them, certenly, were summewhat to nere.[3]
        My fadyr Mercy avysyde me to be of a goode chere         *advised*
        Ande agayn my enmys manly for to fyght.                  *against; to fight manly*

405    I shall convycte them, I hope, everychon.                 *overcome; everyone*
        Yet I say amysse, I do yt not alon.                      *incorrectly*
        Wyth the helpe of the grace of Gode I resyst my fon      *foes*
        Ande ther malycyuse herte.                               *their malicious*
        Wyth my spade I wyll departe, my worschyppull soverence,
410    Ande lyve ever wyth labure to corecte my insolence.       *pride*

---

[1] *I.e., I can't perform the simplest function because of my injury*

[2] *The Lord saveth not with sword and spear: [for it is his battle, and he will deliver you into our hands]*
(1 Kings 17:47)

[3] *For some of them, truly, were a bit too near (i.e., and paid the price)*

I shall go fett corn for my londe; I prey yow of pacyence;                *fetch grain*
Ryght son I shall reverte.                                                 *soon; return*

[*Mankind exits to get his seed; Mischief enters*]

**MISCHIEF**   Alas, alasse, that ever I was wrought!                       *made*
Alasse the whyll, I am wers then nought!                                    *this moment; nothing*
415     Sythyn I was here, by hym that me bought,                           *Since*
I am utterly ondon!                                                         *undone*
I, Myscheff, was here at the begynnynge of the game
Ande arguyde wyth Mercy, Gode gyff hym schame!
He hath taught Mankynde, wyll I have be vane,                               *while; absent*
420     To fyght manly ageyn hys fon.                                       *foes*

For wyth hys spade, that was hys wepyn,
New Gyse, Nowadays, Nought hath all to-beton.                               *severely beaten*
I have grett pyté to se them wepyn.                                         *weeping*
Wyll ye lyst? I here them crye.                                            *listen*

            *Clamant.*                                                      *They cry out*

425     Alasse, alasse! Cum hether, I shall be yowr borow.                  *hither; protector*
Alac, alac! Ven, ven! Cum hethere wyth sorowe!                             *Come*
Pesse, fayer babys, ye shall have a nappyll to-morow![1]
Why grete ye so, why?                                                       *wail*

[*New Guise, Nowadays, and Nought reenter in great pain*]

**NEW GYSE**   Alasse, master, alasse, my privyté!                         *privates (testicles)*
**MISCHIEF**   A, wher? Alake! Fayer babe, ba me!                          *kiss me*
431     Abyde! To son I shall yt se.                                       *see it (i.e., your privates)*
**NOWADAYS**   Here, here, se my hede, goode master!
**MISCHIEF**   Lady, helpe! Sely darlynge, ven, ven!                       *Poor; come*
I shall helpe thee of thi peyn;                                            *heal*
435     I shall smytt of thi hede and sett yt on agayn.                    *smite off*
**NOUGHT**   By owr Lady, ser, a fayer playster![2]

Wyll ye of wyth hys hede! Yt ys a schreude charme!                         *off with; severe treatment*
As for me, I have non harme.                                               *injury*
I were loth to forbere myn arme.                                           *would be reluctant; lose*
440     Ye pley *in nomine patris*, choppe!                                *in the name of the father*
**NEW GYSE**   Ye shall not choppe my jewellys, and I may.                 *testicles; if I can [stop you]*
**NOWADAYS**   Ye, Cristys crose, wyll ye smyght my hede awey?            *Christ's cross; chop*

---

[1] *Peace, sweet babes, you shall have an apple tomorrow (i.e., things will improve)*

[2] *Please give me a plaster bandage (i.e., rather than an amputation)*

Ther wer on and on!¹ Oute! Ye shall not assay. *attempt it*

444     I myght well be callyde a foppe. *fool*

**MISCHIEF**   I kan choppe yt of and make yt agayn. *it off; restore*

**NEW GYSE**   I hade a schreude *recumbentibus* but I fele no peyn. *knockout blow; feel no pain*

**NOWADAYS**   Ande my hede ys all save and holl agayn. *safe and whole*

Now towchynge the mater of Mankynde, *regarding; matter*

Lett us have an interleccyon, sythen ye be cum hethere. *consultation, since*

450     Yt were goode to have an ende. *conclusion*


**MISCHIEF**   How, how, a mynstrell! Know ye ony out? *any at all*

**NOUGHT**   I kan pype in a Walsyngham wystyll, I, Nought, Nought. *whistle*

**MISCHIEF**   Blowe apase, and thou shall bryng hym in wyth a flewte. *now; flute*


[*Nought begins to play*]


**TITIVILLUS**   [*from offstage*] I com wyth my leggys under me.

**MISCHIEF**   How, New Gyse, Nowadays, herke or I goo! *listen before*

456     When owr hedys wer togethere I spake of *si dedero*. *if I give*

**NEW GYSE**   Ye, go thi wey! We shall gather mony onto, *unto [that purpose]*

Ellys ther shall no man hym se. *him (i.e., Titivillus)*

[*to the audience*] Now gostly to owr purpos, worschypfull soverence, *faithfully*

460     We intende to gather mony, yf yt plesse yowr neclygence,

For a man wyth a hede that ys of grett omnipotens.

**NOWADAYS**   Kepe yowr tayll, in goodnes I prey yow, goode brother! *tally (account)*

He ys a worschyppull man, sers, savyng yowr reverens. *He (i.e., Titivillus)*

He lovyth no grotys, nor pens or to pens. *groats; pence or two-pence*

465     Gyf us rede reyallys yf ye wyll se hys abhomynabull presens. *gold royals*

**NEW GYSE**   Not so! Ye that mow not pay the ton, pay the tother.²


At the goodeman of this house fyrst we wyll assay. *To the master; try*

Gode blysse yow, master! Ye say as yll, yet ye wyll not sey nay.³

Lett us go by and by and do them pay. *here and there; make them pay*

470     Ye pay all alyke; well mut ye fare! *may you fare well (as you pay)*

**NOUGHT**   I sey, New Gyse, Nowadays: "*Estis vos pecuniatus?*" *Are you well-moneyed*

I have cryede a fayer wyll, I beschrew yowr patus! *begged; while; curse; head*

**NOWADAYS**   *Ita vere, magister.*⁴ Cumme forth now yowr gatus! *your way (i.e., from your gates)*

474     He ys a goodly man, sers; make space and beware! *sirs*


[*Enter Titivillus*]

---

¹ *There would be one (body) here and one (head) there*

² *Not so! You who may not pay the one, pay the other*

³ *God bless you, master! Though you speak ill of us, you will not say no [to payment]*

⁴ *Therefore truly, master*

**TITIVILLUS**   [*to the audience*] *Ego sum dominancium dominus,*[1] and my name ys Titivillus.

Ye that have goode hors, to yow I sey *caveatis!*            *horse; beware*

Here ys an abyll felyschyppe to tryse hem out at yowr gatys.[2]

         *Loquitur ad New Gyse:*                           *He says to*

         *Ego probo sic*: Ser New Gys, lende me a peny!      *I prove it (their dishonesty) thus*

**NEW GYSE**   I have a grett purse, ser, but I have no monay.

480     By the masse, I fayll to farthyngys of an halpeny;      *two; (i.e., I have nothing)*

        Yyt hade I ten pound this nyght that was.            *Yet; last night*

         *Loquitur ad Nowadays.*                            *He says to*

**TITIVILLUS**   What ys in thi purse? Thou art a stout felow.

**NOWADAYS**   The Devll have thee qwytt! I am a clen jentyllman.[3]

        I prey Gode I be never wers storyde then I am.         *provided for than*

485     Yt shall be otherwyse, I hope, or this nyght passe.           *before*

         *Loquitur ad Nought.*                               *He says to*

**TITIVILLUS**   Herke now! I say thou hast many a peny.            *Listen*

**NOUGHT**   *Non nobis, domine, non nobis,*[4] by Sent Deny!        *Saint Denis*

        The Devll may daunce in my purse for ony peny;    *any (i.e., there's lots of room there)*

489     Yt ys as clen as a byrdys ars.             *clean as a bird's arse*

**TITIVILLUS**   [*to the audience*] Now I say yet ageyn, *caveatis!*        *beware*

        Her ys an abyll felyschyppe to tryse hem out of yowr gatys.    *steal them (your horses)*

        Now I sey, New Gyse, Nowadays, and Nought,

        Go and serche the contré, anon yt be sowghte,         *it will be seen*

        Summe here, summe ther, what yf ye may cache owghte.[5]

495     Yf ye fayll of hors, take what ye may ellys.        *fail to get; else*

**NEW GYSE**   Then speke to Mankynde for the *recumbentibus* of my jewellys.   *blow to my testicles*

**NOWADAYS**   Remember my brokyn hede in the worschyppe of the fyve vowellys.

**NOUGHT**   Ye, goode ser, and the sytyca in my arme.          *sciatica*

**TITIVILLUS**   I know full well what Mankynde dyde to yow.

500     Myschyff hat informyde of all the matere thorow.          *thoroughly*

        I shall venge yowr quarell, I make Gode a vow.

        Forth, and espye were ye may do harme.         *Go forth and spy where*

---

[1] *I am the lord of lords.* See Deuteronomy 10:17, Revelation 19:16.

[2] *Here is a handy company of men (i.e., Nought, New Guise, and Nowadays) to snatch them (i.e., the horses) at your gates*

[3] *May the Devil requite thee! I am a penniless gentleman*

[4] *Not to us, O Lord, not to us [but to thy name give glory]* (Psalm 113:9)

[5] *Some here, some there, to see if you can get anything*

Take William Fyde, yf ye wyll have ony mo.                                            *any more*
I sey, New Gyse, wethere art thou avysyde to go?                                      *where do you plan to go*

**NEW GYSE**  Fyrst I shall begyn at Master Huntyngton of Sauston,
506      Fro thens I shall go to Wylliam Thurlay of Hauston,
         Ande so forth to Pycharde of Trumpyngton.
         I wyll kepe me to thes thre.
**NOWADAYS**  I shall goo to Wyllyham Baker of Waltom,
510      To Rycherde Bollman of Gayton;
         I shall spare Master Woode of Fullburn,
         He ys a *noli me tangere.*                                                   *touch me not (John 20:17)*

**NOUGHT**  I shall goo to Wyllyam Patryke of Massyngham,
         I shall spare Master Alyngton of Botysam
515      Ande Hamonde of Soffeham,
         For drede of *in manus tuas* — qweke.                                        *into Thy hands*
         Felous, cum forth, and go we hens togethyr.                                  *Fellows*
**NEW GYSE**  Syth we shall go, lett us be well ware wethere,                         *Since; aware whither*
         If we may be take, we com no more hethyr.
520      Lett us con well owr neke-verse, that we have not a cheke.                    *recite; problem (see note)*

**TITIVILLUS**  Goo yowr wey, a devll wey, go yowr wey all!                           *the devil's way*
         I blysse yow wyth my lyfte honde: foull yow befall!                          *left; may bad luck be yours*
         Com agayn, I werne, as son as I yow call,                                    *advise, as soon*
         And brynge yowr avantage into this place.                                    *your booty*

         *Exeunt. Manet Titivillus*                                                   *They exit. Titivillus remains*

525      To speke wyth Mankynde I wyll tary here this tyde                            *wait here a while*
         Ande assay hys goode purpose for to sett asyde.                              *try; distract*
         The goode man Mercy shall no lenger be hys gyde.                             *guide*
         I shall make hym to dawnce another trace.                                    *dance another step*

         Ever I go invysybull, yt ys my jett,                                         *fashion*
530      Ande befor hys ey thus I wyll hange my nett                                  *eye*
         To blench hys syght; I hope to have hys fote-mett.                           *deceive; take his measure*
         To yrke hym of hys labur I shall make a frame.                              *make him irked with; scheme*
         Thys borde shall be hyde under the erth prevely;                            *board; hidden; secretly*

         [*Places a board under the earth Mankind has been tilling*]

         Hys spade shall enter, I hope, onredyly;                                     *with difficulty*
535      Be then he hath assayde, he shall be very angry                             *After he has attempted it*
         Ande lose hys pacyens, peyn of schame.                                       *on penalty of shame*
         I shall menge hys corne wyth drawke and wyth durnell;                        *mix; cockle; darnel (weeds)*
         Yt shall not be lyke to sow nor to sell.                                     *fit*

|  | Yondyr he commyth; I prey of cownsell. | *please keep my secret* |
| 540 | He shall wene grace were wane. | *think [that his]; lost* |

*[Enter Mankind with his seed]*

**MANKYNDE**   Now Gode of hys mercy sende us of Hys sonde!                         *guidance*
I have brought sede here to sow wyth my londe.
Qwyll I overdylew yt, here yt shall stonde.                *While I till and cover it over*

*[Sets down the seed, which Titivillus promptly snatches]*

*In nomine Patris et Filii et Spiritus Sancti* now I wyll begyn.[1]

*[He begins to dig, but strikes the board]*

| 545 | Thys londe ys so harde yt makyth unlusty and yrke. | *[one] weary and annoyed* |
|  | I shall sow my corn at wynter and lett Gode werke! | *by chance* |

*[He looks to pick up his seed]*

Alasse, my corn ys lost! Here ys a foull werke!
I se well by tyllynge lytyll shall I wyn.                    *by tilling I shall gain little*
Here I gyff uppe my spade for now and for ever.

*Here Titivillus goth out wyth the spade*

| 550 | To occupye my body I wyll not put me in dever. | *I will not endeavor* |
|  | I wyll here my evynsonge here or I dyssever. | *before I leave* |
|  | Thys place I assyng as for my kyrke. | *assign; church* |
|  | Here in my kerke I knell on my kneys. | *knees* |
|  | *Pater noster qui es in celis.*[2] |  |
| **TITIVILLUS** | [*reentering*] I promes yow I have no lede on my helys. | *lead in my heels* |
| 556 | I am here ageyn to make this felow yrke. | *annoyed* |

| | Qwyst! Pesse! I shall go to hys ere and tytyll therin. | *Shush; whisper* |
|  | A schorte preyere thyrlyth hewyn; of thi preyere blyn. | *pierces; cease* |
|  | Thou art holyer then ever was ony of thi kyn. |  |
| 560 | Aryse and avent thee! Nature compellys. | *relieve yourself* |
| **MANKYNDE** | I wyll into thi yerde, soverens, and cum ageyn son. |  |
|  | For drede of the colyke and eke of the ston | *also; kidney stone* |
|  | I wyll go do that nedys must be don. |  |
|  | My bedys shall be here for whosummever wyll ellys. | *rosary (prayer beads)* |

---

[1] *In the name of the Father and of the Son and of the Holy Spirit, now I will begin*

[2] *Our Father who art in heaven* (Matthew 6:9–15)

      *[Throws down the rosary beads.] Exiat*                      *Exits*

**TITIVILLUS**  Mankynde was besy in hys prayere, yet I dyde hym aryse.     *made*
566    He ys conveyde, be Cryst, from hys dyvyn servyce.         *distracted*
       Wethere ys he, trow ye? Iwysse I am wonder wyse;     *Truly; baffled*
       I have sent hym forth to schyte lesynges.             *shit lies*
       Yff ye have ony sylver, in happe pure brasse,
570    Take a lytyll powder of Parysch and cast over hys face,
       Ande ewyn in the howll-flyght let hym passe.[1]    *even in the owl flight (i.e., at twilight)*
       Titivillus kan lerne yow many praty thyngys.        *teach; crafty*

       I trow Mankynde wyll cum ageyn son,             *believe*
       Or ellys I fere me evynsonge wyll be don.     *evening prayer; done*
575    Hys bedys shall be trysyde asyde, and that anon.   *tossed aside; right away*
       Ye shall a goode sport yf ye wyll abyde.     *shall [be shown]; stay*
       Mankynde cummyth ageyn, well fare he!
       I shall answere hym *ad omnia quare*.        *to every question*
       Ther shall be sett abroche a clerycall mater.  *stirred up a clerical matter (i.e., a debate)*
580    I hope of hys purpose to sett hym asyde.

     *[Mankind reenters]*

**MANKYNDE**  Evynsong hath be in the saynge, I trow, a fayer wyll.  *for a good while*
       I am yrke of yt; yt ys to longe be on myle.    *weary; too long by a mile*
       Do wey! I wyll no more so oft over the chyrche-style.  *not go often over the church stile*
       Be as be may, I shall do another.        *Regardless; otherwise*
585    Of laboure and preyer, I am nere yrke of both;       *nearly*
       I wyll no more of yt, thow Mercy be wroth.    *want; though; angry*
       My hede ys very hevy, I tell yow forsoth.        *truly*
       I shall slepe full my bely and he wore my brother.[2]

     *[He falls asleep]*

**TITIVILLUS**  Ande ever ye dyde, for me kepe now yowr sylence.      *If*
590    Not a worde, I charge yow, peyn of forty pens.    *on penalty of*
       A praty game shall be scheude yow or ye go hens.  *shown you before*
       Ye may here hym snore; he ys sade aslepe.       *sound*
       Qwyst! Pesse! The Devll ys dede! I shall goo ronde in hys ere.  *whisper*
       Alasse, Mankynde, alasse! Mercy stown a mere!  *has stolen a mare*
595    He ys runn away fro hys master, ther wot no man where;  *no one knows*
       Moreover, he stale both a hors and a nete.      *cow (or ox)*

---

[1] Lines 569–71: *If you have a piece of [what you would like to pass off as] silver, perhaps it is pure brass (i.e., coins), / Take a little powder of Paris and sprinkle it over the [coin's] face, / And at twilight the brass coin will pass as silver*

[2] *I shall sleep to my belly's content even if he were my brother (i.e., regardless of circumstance)*

But yet I herde sey he brake hys neke as he rode in Fraunce;                    *broke*
But I thynke he rydyth on the galous, to lern for to daunce,[1]
Bycause of hes theft, that ys hys governance.                                   *conduct*
600  Trust no more on hym, he ys a marryde man.                                 *in; ruined*
Mekyll sorow wyth thi spade beforn thou hast wrought.                           *Much; earlier*
Aryse and aske mercy of New Gyse, Nowadays, and Nought.
Thei cun avyse thee for the best; lett ther goode wyll be sought,
And thi own wyff brethell, and take thee a lemman.                              *deceive; lover (mistress)*

605  Farwell, everychon, for I have don my game,                                *everyone*
For I have brought Mankynde to myscheff and to schame.

          [*Exit. Mankind awakes*]

**MANKYNDE**  Whope who! Mercy hath brokyn hys neke-kycher, avows,              *neck*
Or he hangyth by the neke hye uppon the gallouse.
Adew, fayer masters! I wyll hast me to the ale-house                           *tavern*
610  Ande speke wyth New Gyse, Nowadays, and Nought
And geett me a lemman wyth a smattrynge face.                                   *lover; kissable*

          [*Enter New Guise through the audience*]

**NEW GYSE**  Make space, for cokkys body sakyrde, make space!                 *Christ's sacred body*
A ha! Well overron! Gode gyff hym evyll grace!                                 *escaped*
We were nere Sent Patrykes Wey, by Hym that me bought.                         *near; Him (i.e., Christ)*

615  I was twychyde by the neke; the game was begunne.
A grace was, the halter brast asonder: *ecce signum*![2]
The halff ys abowte my neke; we hade a nere rune!                             *half [of the noose]; close call*
"Beware," quod the goodewyff when sche smot of here husbondys hede,"beware!"[3]

Myscheff ys a convicte, for he coude hys neke-verse.                           *knew*
620  My body gaff a swynge when I hynge uppon the casse.                       *hang upon; gallows*
Alasse, he wyll hange such a lyghly man, and a fers,                           *handsome; fierce*
For stelynge of an horse, I prey Gode gyf hym care!

Do wey this halter! What devll doth Mankynde here, wyth sorow!  *Get rid of; What the*
624  Alasse, how my neke ys sore, I make avowe!                                *I swear*
**MANKYNDE**  Ye be welcom, New Gyse! Ser, what chere wyth yow?                *how are you*
**NEW GYSE**  Well ser, I have no cause to morn.
**MANKYNDE**  What was that abowte yowr neke, so Gode yow amende?
**NEW GYSE**  In feyth, Sent Audyrs holy bende.                                *St. Audrey's; band*

---

[1] *But I think he rides on the gallows, to learn how to dance (i.e., he quivers as he hangs)*

[2] *As luck would have it, the noose broke in two: behold the proof*

[3] *"Beware," said the good wife when she smote off her husband's head, "beware!"*

I have a lytyll dyshes, as yt plese Gode to sende,                        *disease*
630      Wyth a runnynge ryngeworme.

        [*Enter Nowadays through the audience*]

NOWADAYS  Stonde arom, I prey thee, brother myn!                    *Stand back*
        I have laburryde all this nyght; wen shall we go dyn?
        A chyrche her besyde shall pay for ale, brede, and wyn.          *nearby*
634     Lo, here ys stoff wyll serve.                          *that will serve [us] well*
NEW GYSE  Now by the holy Mary, thou art better marchande then I!       *merchant*
NOUGHT  Avante, knawys, lett me go by!                          *Out of my way, knaves*
        I kan not geet and I shulde sterve.[1]

        [*Enter Mischief*]

MISCHIEF  Here cummyth a man of armys! Why stonde ye so styll?
        Of murder and manslawter I have my bely-fyll.
NOWADAYS  What, Myscheff, have ye ben in presun? And yt be yowr wyll,        *If*
641     Me semyth ye have scoryde a peyr of fetters.            *It seems to me; worn out*
MISCHIEF  I was chenyde by the armys: lo, I have them here.
        The chenys I brast asundyr and kyllyde the jaylere,
        Ye, ande hys fayer wyff halsyde in a cornere;                    *ravished*
645     A, how swetly I kyssyde the swete mowth of hers!

        When I hade do, I was myn owyn bottler;                    *was done; own butler*
        I brought awey wyth me both dysch and dublere.                    *platter*
        Here ys anow for me; be of goode chere!                          *enough*
        Yet well fare the new chesance!                          *financial dealing*

        [*They begin to feast, but Mankind interrupts them*]

MANKYNDE  I aske mercy of New Gyse, Nowadays, and Nought.
651     Onys wyth my spade I remember that I faught.
        I wyll make yow amendys yf I hurt yow ought                    *at all*
        Or dyde ony grevaunce.                                    *any*

NEW GYSE  What a devll lykyth thee to be of this dysposycyon?            *makes*
MANKYNDE  I drempt Mercy was hange, this was my vysyon,
656     Ande that to yow thre I shulde have recors and remocyon.      *recourse and resort*
        Now I prey yow hertyly of yowr goode wyll.
        I crye yow mercy of all that I dyde amysse.                    *beg*
NOWADAYS  I sey, New Gys, Nought, Tytivillus made all this:      *put all this in his head*
660     As sekyr as Gode ys in hewyn, so yt ys.                          *surely*
NOUGHT  [*to Mankind*] Stonde uppe on yowr feet! Why stonde ye so styll?

---

[1] *[If] I can not get [some of that food], I shall die*

NEW GYSE  Master Myscheff, we wyll yow exort
        Mankyndys name in yowr bok for to report.
MISCHIEF  I wyll not so; I wyll sett a corte.
665     Nowadays, mak proclamacyon,
        And do yt *sub forma jurys*, dasarde!  — *in legal form, fool*
NOWADAYS  Oyyt! Oyyt! Oyet! All manere of men and comun women  — *Oyez (Hear ye)*
        To the cort of Myschyff othere cum or sen!  — *send [excuses]*
669     Mankynde shall retorn; he ys on of owr men.  — *one of our*
MISCHIEF  Nought, cum forth, thou shall be stewerde.  — *steward (scribe)*

NEW GYSE  Master Myscheff, hys syde gown may be solde.  — *long coat*
        He may have a jakett therof, and mony tolde.  — *money left over*

        *Nought scribit*  — *writes*

MANKYNDE  I wyll do for the best, so I have no colde.  — *as long as*

        [*Mankind takes off his coat*]

        Holde, I prey yow, and take yt wyth yow.
675     Ande let me have yt ageyn in ony wyse.  — *way*
NEW GYSE  I promytt yow a fresch jakett after the new gyse.  — *style*
MANKYNDE  Go and do that longyth to yowr offyce,  — *belongs; duty*
        And spare that ye mow!  — *And salvage what you can*

        [*New Guise exits with Mankind's coat*]

NOUGHT  Holde, master Myscheff, and rede this.
MISCHIEF  Here ys *blottybus in blottis*,  — *(nonsense Latin)*
681     *Blottorum blottibus istis.*  — *(nonsense Latin)*
        I beschrew yowr erys, a fayer hande!  — *curse; written hand*
NOWADAYS  Ye, yt ys a goode rennynge fyst.  — *running fist (cursive writing)*
684     Such an hande may not be myst.  — *neglected*
NOUGHT  I shulde have don better, hade I wyst.  — *known*
MISCHIEF  Take hede, sers, yt stoude you on hande.  — *it should behoove you (punning)*
        [*He reads*] *Carici tenta generalis.*  — *The general court having been held*
        In a place ther goode ale ys
        *Anno regni regitalis*  — *In the regnal year*
690     *Edwardi nullateni*  — *Of Edward the Nothing*
        On yestern day in Feverere — the yere passyth fully,[1]
        As Nought hath wrytyn; here ys owr Tulli,  — *Cicero*
        *Anno regni regis nulli!*  — *In the regnal year of king nobody*

---

[1] *On the last day of February — the year passed fully away*

**NOWADAYS**   What how, New Gyse! Thou makyst moche taryynge.                              *delay*
695        That jakett shall not be worth a ferthynge.                                       *farthing*
**NEW GYSE**   Out of my wey, sers, for drede of fyghtynge!

> [*Reentering through the audience*]

Lo, here ys a feet tayll, lyght to leppe abowte![1]
**NOUGHT**   Yt ys not schapyn worth a morsell of brede;
         Ther ys to moche cloth, yt weys as ony lede.                                        *is as heavy as*
700        I shall goo and mende yt, ellys I wyll lose my hede.                               *alter it; else*
         Make space, sers, lett me go owte.

> [*Exits through the audience with Mankind's coat*]

**MISCHIEF**   Mankynde, cum hethere! God sende yow the gowte!                               *gout*
         Ye shall goo to all the goode felouse in the cuntré aboute;
         Onto the goodewyff when the goodeman ys owte.
705        "I wyll," sey ye.
**MANKYNDE**            I wyll, ser.
**NEW GYSE**   There arn but sex dedly synnys, lechery ys non,                               *six deadly sins*
         As yt may be verefyede be us brethellys everychon.                                  *rascals (villains)*
         Ye shall goo robbe, stell, and kyll, as fast as ye may gon.                         *go*
         "I wyll," sey ye.
**MANKYNDE**            I wyll, ser.
**NOWADAYS**   On Sundays on the morow erly betyme                                           *early in the morning*
711        Ye shall wyth us to the all-house erly to go dyn                                   *alehouse*
         And forbere masse and matens, owres, and prime.[2]
         "I wyll," sey ye.
**MANKYNDE**            I wyll, ser.
**MISCHIEF**   Ye must have be yowr syde a longe *da pacem*,                                 *"give peace" (i.e., a dagger)*
715        As trew men ryde be the wey for to onbrace them,                                  *cut them up*
         Take ther monay, kytt ther throtys, thus overface them.                             *cut; overcome*
         "I wyll," sey ye.
**MANKYNDE**            I wyll, ser.

**NOUGHT**   [*reentering*] Here ys a joly jakett! How sey ye?
**NEW GYSE**   Yt ys a goode jake of fence for a mannys body.                                *tunic*
720        Hay, doog, hay! Whoppe whoo! Go yowr wey lyghtly!
         Ye are well made for to ren.                                                        *run*

> [*Mercy enters to the side*]

---

[1] *Lo, here is a handsome form [of clothing] in which to leap about lively*

[2] *And skip mass and matins, hours, and prime*

**MISCHIEF**   Tydyngys, tydyngys! I have aspyede on!                           *seen one (i.e., Mercy)*
               Hens wyth yowr stuff, fast we were gon!                          *stolen goods, let's go quickly*
724            I beschrew the last shall com to hys hom.                        *curse; last one who*

               Amen! *Dicant omnes.*                                           *Let them all say*

**MERCY**  What how, Mankynde! Fle that felyschyppe, I yow prey!                *Run away from that gang*
**MANKYNDE**   I shall speke wyth thee another tyme, to-morn, or the next day.
               We shall goo forth together to kepe my faders yer-day.          *anniversary of his death*
               A tapster, a tapster! Stow, statt, stow!                        *tapster (innkeeper)*
**MISCHIEF**  A myscheff go wyth! Here I have foull fall.                       *with you; a bad fall*
731           Hens, awey fro me, or I shall beschyte yow all.                  *beshit*
**NEW GYSE**   What how, ostlere, hostlere! Lende us a football!               *innkeeper*
               Whoppe whow! Anow, anow, anow, anow!

               [*After much play, in which Mercy is trampled, they exit. Mercy remains*]

**MERCY**  My mynde ys dyspersyde, my body trymmelyth as the aspen leffe.       *trembles; leaf*
735            The terys shuld trekyll down by my chekys, were not yowr reverrence.[1]
               Yt were to me solace, the cruell vysytacyon of deth.            *death would be a comfort*
               Wythout rude behaver I kan not expresse this inconvenyens.      *misfortune*
               Wepynge, sythynge, and sobbynge were my suffycyens.            *sighing; sustenance*
               All naturall nutriment to me as caren ys odybull.               *carrion; odious*
740            My inwarde afflixcyon yeldyth me tedyouse unto yowr presens.    *makes*
               I kan not bere yt evynly that Mankynde ys so flexybull.         *calmly; easily swayed*
               Man onkynde, wherever thou be! For all this world was not aprehensyble
               To dyscharge thin orygynall offence, thraldam, and captyvyté,
               Tyll Godys own welbelovyde son was obedient and passyble.[2]
745            Every droppe of hys bloode was schede to purge thin iniquité.   *your (thine)*
               I dyscomende and dysalow thin oftyn mutabylyté.                 *moral changeability*
               To every creature thou art dyspectouse and odyble.             *despicable; odious*
               Why art thou so oncurtess, so inconsyderatt? Alasse, who ys me! *uncourteous*
               As the fane that turnyth wyth the wynde, so thou art convertyble.[3]

750            In trust ys treson;[4] thi promes ys not credyble;
               Thy perversyose ingratytude I cannot rehers.                    *perverse; describe*
               To God and to all the holy corte of hewyn thou art despectyble, *contemptible*
               As a nobyll versyfyer makyth mencyon in this verse:

---

[1] *The tears should trickle down my face, if it were not for your (the audience's) reverence*

[2] Lines 742–44: *Unnatural Mankind, wherever you are! For all this world was not able / To atone for your orginal sin, thralldom, and captivity [by the flesh], / Until God's own well-beloved son was obedient and willing to suffer*

[3] *Like the weather vane that turns with the wind, you too are changeable*

[4] *In trusting you, I have only found betrayal*

"*Lex et natura, Cristus et omnia jura*
755     *Damnant ingratum, lugent eum fore natum.*"[1]

O goode Lady and Mother of mercy, have pety and compassyon          (*i.e., Virgin Mary*)
Of the wrechydnes of Mankynde, that ys so wanton and so frayll!                *On*
Lett mercy excede justyce, dere Mother, amytt this supplycacyon,          *admit (hear)*
Equyté to be leyde onparty and Mercy to prevayll.[2]

760     To sensuall lyvynge ys reprovable, that ys nowadays,
As be the comprehence of this mater yt may be specyfyede.[3]
New Gyse, Nowadays, Nought wyth ther allectuose ways               *alluring*
They have pervertyde Mankynde, my swet sun, I have well espyede.     *sweet son; seen*

A, wyth thes cursyde caytyfs, and I may, he shall not long indure.[4]
765     I, Mercy, hys father gostly, wyll procede forth and do my propyrté.     *spiritual; duty*
Lady, helpe! This maner of lyvynge ys a detestabull plesure.
*Vanitas vanitatum*, all ys but a vanyté.               *Vanity of vanities (Ecclesiastes 1:2)*

Mercy shall never be convicte of hys oncurtes condycyon.[5]
Wyth wepynge terys be nygte and be day I wyll goo and never sesse.
770     Shall I not fynde hym? Yes, I hope. Now Gode be my proteccyon!
My predylecte son, where be ye? Mankynde, *ubi es?*          *most beloved; where are you*

[*Exit. Enter Mischief; the others are offstage relieving themselves*]

**MISCHIEF**   My prepotent fadere, when ye sowpe, sowpe out yowr messe.[6]
Ye are all to-gloryede in yowr termys; ye make many a lesse.          *too-fancy; lie*
Wyll ye here? He cryeth ever "Mankynde, *ubi es?*"          *hear; where are you*
**NEW GYSE**   *Hic hyc, hic hic, hic hic, hic hic!*
776     That ys to sey, here, here, here! Ny dede in the cryke.          *Near(ly) dead in the creek*
Yf ye wyll have hym, goo and syke, syke, syke!               *sigh, seek (pun)*
Syke not overlong, for losynge of yowr mynde!

**NOWADAYS**   Yf ye wyll have Mankynde, how *domine, domine, dominus!*          *O Lord, Lord, Lord*
780     Ye must speke to the schryve for a *cape corpus*,     *sheriff; "take the body" (a writ of arrest)*

---

[1] Lines 754–55: *Law and nature, Christ and all justice / Condemn the ungrateful one; they lament that he would ever be born*

[2] *Let Equity (Justice) be laid aside and Mercy prevail*

[3] Lines 760–61: *Sensual living is to blame for what takes place nowadays, / As may be demonstrated by an understanding of this situation*

[4] *With these cursed slaves [of the flesh], if I can do anything about it, he shall not [have to] endure long*

[5] *Mercy shall never be frustrated by his (i.e., Mankind's) bad habits*

[6] *My most powerful father (i.e., Mercy), when you sup, drink/eat your fill*

Ellys ye must be fayn to retorn wyth *non est inventus*.                    *it is not found*
How sey ye, ser? My bolte ys schett.                                        *has been shot*
**NOUGHT**   I am doynge of my nedyngys; beware how ye schott![1]
Fy, fy, fy! I have fowll arayde my fote.                                    *foully dirtied my foot*
785   Be wyse for schotynge wyth yowr takyllys, for Gode wott    *shooting; weapons; knows*
My fote ys fowly overschett.                                                *covered with shit*

**MISCHIEF**   A parlement, a parlement! Cum forth, Nought, behynde.        *Let's confer*
A cownsell belyve! I am aferde Mercy wyll hym fynde.           *counsel quickly; afraid*
How sey ye, and what sey ye? How shall we do wyth Mankynde?
**NEW GYSE**   Tysche! A flyes weyng! Wyll ye do well?              *fly's wing (a small matter)*
791   He wenyth Mercy were honge for stelyng of a mere.                    *thinks; mare*
Myscheff, go sey to hym that Mercy sekyth everywere.
He wyll honge hymselff, I undyrtake, for fere.                       *He (i.e., Mankind)*
**MISCHIEF**   I assent therto; yt ys wyttyly seyde and well.                 *wittily*

**NOWADAYS**   [*to New Gyse*] Qwyppe yt in thi cote; anon yt were don.[2]
796   Now Sent Gabryellys modyr save the clothes of thi schon!   *Saint Gabriel's mother; shoes*
All the bokys in the worlde, yf thei hade be undon,                   *opened [and read]*
Kowde not a cownselde us bett.                               *Could not have advised us better*

*Hic exit Myscheff* [*who then returns with Mankind*]                         *Here*

**MISCHIEF**   How, Mankynde! Cumm and speke wyth Mercy, he is here fast by.    *near by*
**MANKYNDE**   A roppe, a rope, a rope! I am not worthy.
**MISCHIEF**   Anon, anon, anon! I have yt here redy,
802   Wyth a tre also that I have gett.                                 *gallows tree; gotten*

Holde the tre, Nowadays, Nought! Take hede and be wyse!
**NEW GYSE**   Lo, Mankynde! Do as I do; this ys thi new gyse.                  *fashion*
805   Gyff the roppe just to thy neke; this ys myn avyse.             *Set; just so; advice*

[*Mercy reenters with a whip, chasing Mischief*]

**MISCHIEF**   Helpe thisylff, Nought! Lo, Mercy ys here!
He skaryth us wyth a bales; we may no lengere tary.            *scares; whip; remain*

[*They run off, leaving New Guise hanging*]

**NEW GYSE**   Qweke, qweke, qweke! Alass, my thrott! I beschrew yow, mary!    *curse; indeed*
A, Mercy, Crystys coppyde curse go wyth yow, and Sent Davy!   *heaped-up; Saint David*
810   Alasse, my wesant! Ye were sumwhat to nere.                    *throat; too close*

---

[1] *Beware how you shoot while I am moving my bowels*

[2] *Hide it (i.e., the noose) in your coat; it should be done quickly*

*Exiant*                                                                    *They exit*

[*The Vices return to save New Guise, but leave behind Mankind, who grovels on the ground before Mercy*]

**MERCY** Aryse, my precyose redempt son! Ye be to me full dere.

He ys so tymerouse, me semyth hys vytall spryt doth exspyre.     *timorous, it seems to me*

**MANKYNDE** Alasse, I have be so bestyally dysposyde, I dare not apere.

To se yowr solaycyose face I am not worthy to desyere.     *comforting*

**MERCY** Yowr crymynose compleynt wondyth my hert as a lance.     *guilty lament wounds*

816     Dyspose yowrsylff mekly to aske mercy, and I wyll assent.

Yelde me nethyr golde nor tresure, but yowr humbyll obeysyance,     *obedience*

The voluntary sujeccyon of yowr hert, and I am content.

**MANKYNDE** What, aske mercy yet onys agayn? Alas, yt were a vyle petycyun.     *petition*

820     Evyr to offend and ever to aske mercy, yt ys a puerilité.     *puerility (childish behavior)*

Yt ys so abhominabyll to rehers my iterat transgrescion     *repeated*

I am not worthy to have mercy be no possibilité.     *by*

**MERCY** O, Mankend, my singler solas, this is a lamentabyll excuse.     *singular solace*

The dolorous terys of my hert, how thei begyn to amownt!

825     O pirssid Jhesu, help thou this synfull synner to redouce!     *wounded; reform*

*Nam hec est mutacio dextre Excelsi; vertit impios et non sunt.*[1]

Aryse and aske mercy, Mankend, and be associat to me.     *allied*

Thy deth schall be my hevynesse; alas, tys pety yt schuld be thus.     *it is a pity*

Thy obstinacy wyll exclude thee fro the glorius perpetuité.     *from the eternal glory*

830     Yet for my lofe ope thy lyppys and sey "*Miserere mei, Deus!*"[2]     *love*

**MANKYNDE** The egall justyse of God wyll not permytte such a synfull wrech     *equitable*

To be revyvyd and restoryd ageyn; yt were impossibyll.

**MERCY** The justyce of God wyll as I wyll, as Hymselfe doth preche:

*Nolo mortem peccatoris, inquit,* yff he wyll be redusyble.[3]

**MANKYNDE** Than mercy, good Mercy! What ys a man wythowte mercy?

836     Lytyll ys our parte of paradyse were mercy ne were.     *where there is no mercy*

Good Mercy, excuse the inevytabyll objeccion of my gostly enmy.

The proverbe seyth, "the trewth tryith the sylfe." Alas, I have mech care.

**MERCY** God wyll not make yow prevy onto hys last jugement.

840     Justyce and Equité shall be fortyfyid, I wyll not denye.     *fortified*

---

[1] *For the right hand of the Lord is changed; the wicked are overthrown and are no more.* See Psalm 76:11 and Proverbs 12:7.

[2] *Have mercy on me, my God* (Psalms 50:3, 55:3, and 56:2)

[3] *[As I live,] saith the Lord God, I desire not the death of the wicked, [but that the wicked turn from his way, and live]* (Ezechiel 33:11), providing he (the sinner) desires to be redeemed.

Trowthe may not so cruelly procede in hys streyt argument                        *strict*
But that Mercy schall rewle the mater wythowte contraversye.    *However; undoubtedly*

Aryse now and go wyth me in thys deambulatorye.                                 *walkway*
Inclyne yowyr capacité; my doctrine ys convenient.                              *relevant*
845    Synne not in hope of mercy; that is a cryme notary.                         *notorious*
To truste overmoche in a prince yt ys not expedient.

In hope when ye syn ye thynke to have mercy, beware of that aventure.
The good Lord seyd to the lecherus woman of Chanane,
The holy gospell ys the autorité, as we rede in scrypture,                      *authority*
850    "*Vade et iam amplius noli peccare.*"[1]

Cryst preservyd this synfull woman takeyn in avowtry;                           *adultery*
He seyde to here theis wordys, "Go and syn no more."                            *listen to*
So to yow, go and syn no more.  Beware of veyn confidens of mercy;              *vain*
Offend not a prince on trust of hys favour, as I seyd before.
855    Yf ye fele yoursylffe trappyd in the snare of your gostly enmy,
Aske mercy anon; beware of the contynuance.                          *persisting in sin*
Whyll a wond ys fresch yt ys provyd curabyll be surgery,                        *wound*
That yf yt procede ovyrlong, yt ys cawse of gret grevans.                       *grievance*

**MANKYNDE**    To aske mercy and to have, this ys a lyberall possescion.       *generous gift*
860    Schall this expedycius petycion ever be alowyd, as ye have insyght?
**MERCY**  In this present lyfe mercy ys plenté, tyll deth makyth hys dyvysion;    *division*
But whan ye be go, *usque ad minimum quadrantem* ye schall rekyn your ryght.[2]
Aske mercy and have, whyll the body wyth the sowle hath hys annexion;           *union*
Yf ye tary tyll your dyscesse, ye may hap of your desyre to mysse.[3]
865    Be repentant here, trust not the owr of deth; thynke on this lessun:       *hour*
"*Ecce nunc tempus acceptabile, ecce nunc dies salutis.*"[4]

All the vertu in the word yf ye myght comprehend                               *world*
Your merytys were not premyabyll to the blys above,            *merits would not earn you*
Not to the lest joy of hevyn, of your propyr efforte to ascend.
870    Wyth mercy ye may; I tell yow no fabyll, scrypture doth prove.[5]

---

[1] *Go, and now sin no more* (John 8:11)

[2] *But when you are gone (i.e., dead) you must calculate your reward up to the least fraction of a coin*

[3] *If you delay until your death, you may by chance through your will lose (i.e., your chance for mercy)*

[4] *Behold, now is the acceptable time; behold, now is the day of salvation* (2 Corinthians 6:2)

[5] Lines 867–70: *Even if you could come to know all the virtue in the world, / Your merits would not bring you to heavenly bliss, / Nor to the least joy of heaven, by your own effort to ascend there. / With mercy you may [gain heavenly bliss]; I tell you no fable, scripture proves it*

**MANKYNDE**   O Mercy, my suavius solas and synguler recreatory,[1]
My predilecte specyall, ye are worthy to have my love;    *chosen beloved*
For wythowte deserte and menys supplicatorie    *means of supplication*
Ye be compacient to my inexcusabyll reprove.    *compassionate; shame*

875   A, yt swemyth my hert to thynk how onwysely I have wroght.    *grieves; unwisely; sinned*
Tytivillus, that goth invisibele, hyng hys nett before my eye    *goes; hung*
And by hys fantasticall visionys sediciusly sowght,    *sought [to destroy me]*
To New Gyse, Nowadayis, Nowght causyd me to obey.

**MERCY**   Mankend, ye were oblivyows of my doctrine monytorye.    *forgetful; admonitory*
880   I seyd before, Titivillus wold asay yow a bronte.    *attempt an attack on you*
Beware fro hensforth of hys fablys delusory.
The proverbe seyth, "*Jacula prestita minus ledunt.*"    *Darts anticipated hurt less*

Ye have thre adversaryis and he ys mayster of hem all:
That ys to sey, the Devell, the World, the Flesch and the Fell.    *skin*
885   The New Gyse, Nowadayis, Nowgth, the World we may hem call;
And propyrly Titivillus syngnyfyth the fend of helle;    *fiend*

The Flesch, that ys the unclene concupissens of your body.    *unclean carnal desire*
These be your thre gostly enmyis, in whom ye have put your confidens.
Thei browt yow to Myscheffe to conclude your temporall glory,
890   As yt hath be schewyd before this worscheppyll audiens.    *been shown*

Remembyr how redy I was to help yow; fro swheche I was not dangerus;[2]
Wherfore, goode sunne, absteyne fro syn evermore after this.
Ye may both save and spyll yowr sowle that ys so precyus.    *destroy*
*Libere welle, libere nolle* God may not deny iwys.[3]

895   Beware of Titivillus wyth his net and of all enmys will,
Of your synfull delectacion that grevyth your gostly substans.    *spiritual being*
Your body ys your enmy; let hym not have hys wyll.
Take your leve whan ye wyll. God send yow good persverans!    *leave*

**MANKYNDE**   Syth I schall departe, blyse me, fader, her then I go.    *Since; bless; before (ere)*
900   God send us all plenté of Hys gret mercy!
**MERCY**   *Dominus custodit te ab omni malo*
*In nomine Patris et Filii et Spiritus Sancti. Amen!*[4]

---

[1] *O Mercy, my sweet solace and sole source of comfort*

[2] *Remember how ready I was to help you; from such [encounters] I was not reluctant*

[3] *Surely, God may not deny you [the choice] to will freely, [or] not to will freely*

[4] Lines 901–02: *The Lord keepeth thee from all evil* [Psalm 120:7] / *In the name of the Father, Son, and Holy Spirit. Amen*

*Hic exit Mankynde*                                                    *Here exits*

Wyrschepyll sofereyns, I have do my propirté:                    *have completed my task*
Mankynd ys deliveryd by my faverall patrocynye.                     *practical protection*
905   God preserve hym fro all wyckyd captivité
And send hym grace hys sensuall condicions to mortifye!                      *habits*

Now for Hys love that for us receyvyd hys humanité,              *took human form*
Serge your condicyons wyth dew examinacion.              *Examine; habits; thorough*
Thynke and remembyr the world ys but a vanité,
910   As yt ys provyd daly by diverse transmutacyon.

Mankend ys wrechyd, he hath sufficyent prove.                    *sufficiently proven*
Therefore God grant yow all *per suam misericordiam*                 *through his mercy*
That ye may be pleyferys wyth the angellys above            *companions (playmates)*
And have to your porcyon *vitam eternam. Amen!*              *for; portion eternal life*


*Fynis.*                                                              *The end*

 **EXPLANATORY NOTES**

ABBREVIATIONS: *CP*: *Castle of Perseverance*; **E**: Eccles, *Mankind* in *Macro Plays*; **L**: Lester, *Mankind* in *Three Late Medieval Morality Plays*; **MED**: *Middle English Dictionary*; **MM**: Digby *Mary Magdalene*; **OED**: *Oxford English Dictionary*; **OI**: *Occupation and Idleness*; **S**: Smart, "Some Notes on *Mankind*;" **s.d.:** stage direction; **W**: *Wisdom*.

| | |
|---|---|
| 1–5 | The opening speech by Mercy is comparable to the openings of several other Middle English plays. See the initial benediction of Mercy to the Primus Vexillator at the beginning of *CP* or to Occupation in *OI*. The gift of creation is a common theme in the openings of *Lucidus and Dubius*, *CP*, and *OI*. As Sikorska points out, the speech itself distances Mercy from "the dramatic action by virtue of its homiletic content," ultimately establishing him as a character who, as a messenger of God, functions as "a persona both inside and outside of the play" ("*Mankind* and the Question of Power Dynamics," p. 204). |
| 1 | E divides the play into three scenes: the first running from the beginning to line 412, the second from 413 to 733, and the third from 734 to 914, the end of the play. |
| 7–16 | According to medieval soteriology, the original sin of Adam made all subsequent human beings prone to sin, and only Christ's sacrifice on the cross enabled salvation. Salvation through Christ's suffering is a common theme in much medieval drama; compare Doctrine in *OI*, lines 203–06, and the opening speeches of Charity in *Youth*, or of Pity and Contemplation in *Hick Scorner*. Such universal themes situate the action within the larger context of human experience as it is shaped by the inevitability of death and the cycle of the sin and repentance, shifting the focus from the concerns or anxieties of specific individuals to those of humanity as a whole. |
| 12 | *lavatorye.* Compare *CP*: "Mercy schal be hys waschynge-well" (line 3145). |
| 17–24 | The opening presentation of Mercy's worthiness mirrors the initial speeches of Wysdom in *W*, Occupacion in *OI*, Charity in *Youth*, and Pity in *Hick Scorner*. Lynn-Dianne Beene notes how Mercy avoids referring to himself in the first person here by pluralizing pronouns to include God the Holy Trintiy, thus emphasizing "the deity rather than the speaker who represents the deity" ("Language Patterns in *Mankind*," p. 25). |
| 22 | *Owr Lady.* The mother of Jesus, Mary, is commonly portrayed in literature and art as a mediator between the deity and humans as well as an advocate for the sinner |

on Judgment Day. Compare *Hick Scorner* "Record I take of Mary, that wept tears of blood" (line 10), and *OI* (lines 823–63).

24      *defendawnte.* Mercy as a protector for the soul adds to the conceit of the soul being defended in a court, especially in the court on Judgment Day.

25      Compare Mercy's exhortation to avoid wickedness to Wisdom's in *W* (lines 109–60), and Occupacion's in *OI* (lines 368–96).

27      *yowr gostly enmy.* The enemy of your soul, i.e., the devil: a small example of the notion that medieval spirituality was often stated in terms of warfare. Compare *Everyman* "For I have a grete enemy that hath me in wayte" (line 334) and "Mundus et Infans" "Now Mary, Moder . . . saue you from our enemy" (lines 753–55).

29      *O ye soverens that sytt and ye brothern that stonde ryght uppe.* Those who sat were the employers and guests of the houses, and those who stood were the servants. Much has been made of the distinction between the two groups, as it gives us a context for the performance: the line makes clear that at least one of the potential venues of the play was in the private household or inn. L parallels Hamlet's reference to the "groundlings" in *Hamlet* III.ii.12 (p. 4).

32–38   The notion of Christ as the head and his followers, or the saints, as the body begins in Colossians 1:18 and 1 Corinthians 12:12–31. Lines 36–38 refer to the blood of Christ as the sacrament. The body was commonly used as a metaphor for society in which every class or profession had a distinct function. Michael J. Preston suggests the worldly devils' preoccupation with crudeness, as opposed to Mercy's elevated rhetoric, and Mankind's vacillation between the two, are best as examples of the variability of human behavior: "we may gaze below the waist (i.e., act like a lower-class person) or — to use the alternative paradigm — gaze according to our lower (baser) desires; at other times we may gaze above the waist, ideally above the shoulders" ("Re-Presentations of (Im)moral Behavior," p. 229).

34      *lykynnyde to a lambe.* Christ is typically referred to as the lamb of God. See John 1:29: "The next day he saw Jesus coming to him and said, "Behold, the Lamb of God who takes away the sin of the world!"

36      *Wyth the precyose rever that runnyth from Hys wombe.* L, following S, limits the meaning to the "blood of Christ as the sacrament," but the sense goes beyond this. The direct reference is to John 19:34, the soldier thrusting his lance into the crucified Christ's side. In medieval interpretation, what flows from Christ's wound is the oil of mercy that originated in the tree of life in the Garden of Eden, then, later, pours forth from Christ's side on the cross. The story is told in the *Cursor Mundi, South English Legendary,* and *Legenda Aurea* and explored in Esther Casier Quinn's *Quest of Seth for the Oil of Mercy* and Charles Mills Gayley's *Plays of Our Forefathers.* The image of the oil of mercy is linked with the line "your name is as oil poured out," the second verse of the Song of Songs, the language of which forms the subtext of the redemption of Mankind: see, for example, lines 811–12 and 871–72.

40      *Of the mortall enmye, that vemynousse serpente.* The devil, who in the shape of a ser-
        pent tempted Eve and Adam. Christ's death remedies the death sentence that
        began with their fall from grace.

43      *The corn shall be savyde, the chaffe shall be brente.* The sources of the corn (grain) and
        chaff metaphor, especially in the context of the Last Judgment, are Matthew 3:12
        and Luke 3:17. See also lines 50, 54–63, 180, and 185 below. Corn is the col-
        lective term for the grain of cereals such as wheat, spelt, rye, barley, rice, etc.,
        but not maize, which was yet to be introduced from the New World. Ashley, on
        the metaphorical significance of the paradigm, asserts: "corn and chaff stand not
        merely for the worthy man and the sinner, but for the kind of words to which each
        gives his allegiance . . . Mercy's job is to persuade us of the crucial distinction
        between corn and chaff, while the Wordlings and Mischief devote their
        considerable wit to obliterating that distinction" ("Battle of Words," p. 132).

45      *calcacyon.* "Preaching." See *MED* "calken" (v.), citing the Paston letters 3.48 on
        a priest who "kalked and reported." Mischief seems to be responding
        sarcastically to Mercy's preaching with its calks on corn and chaff and "prem-
        edytacyons." L and Bevington (*Medieval Drama*) suggest an emendation to
        "calc[ul]acion" but that emendation seems unnecessary. E picks up on the corn-
        and-chaff trope to suggest "threshing," though this sense is not attributed in
        *OED* until 1656. But as a figure of rhetoric, the separation of chaff and grain has
        been a preaching trope for generations as one metaphor is calked to another
        until Mischief objects through mockery.

47      *Yowr wytt ys lytyll, yowr hede ys mekyll.* Mischief suggests that because Mercy's head
        is so filled with his own preaching, his wit is diminished. E and L note the expre-
        ssion "Mickle head, little wit," recorded in Smith and Wilson, eds., *Oxford
        Dictionary of English Proverbs* (p. 422); Whiting, *Proverbs, Sentences, and Proverbial
        Phrases*, H226; and Tilley, *Dictionary of the Proverbs in England*, H245.

49      *Mysse-masche.* Cited in the *OED* as the earliest use of *mish-mash*. E and S attempt
        to explain the origins of this term and the other words in this sequence (e.g.,
        "raffe") as a pun on the noun *raff* (refuse). It is perhaps best to see them simply
        as provocative nonsense verse.

51      *Raffe.* Since "raff" meant "worthless material, trash, refuse" according to S (p.
        57), "Raffe" was considered a lower class and comical name.

52      *Onschett yowr lokke.* "Purse" is not a sense for "lokke" cited in *MED* though it ack-
        nowledges the possibility of a container or strong box. S (p. 57) interprets the
        phrase to mean "to talk, to speak," as in lines 128–29. E's suggestion, "open your
        locked door and give a halfpenny," may be too limiting, as the lock seems to be
        something other than a door — a treasure trove, perhaps. Given the effort of the
        company to collect money later this could be seen as an opening gesture in that
        direction, in which case the "lokke" would be something they have on their
        person, like a purse or wallet.

57      *Corn servit bredibus, chaffe horsibus, straw fyrybusque.* Mischief's mock Latin, which
        means "Corn serves for bread, chaff for horses, and straw for fires," parodies

Mercy's preaching. His mockery undermines the oversimplified either/or model that Mercy offers.

70        *in the devyllys name*. By using the name of the devil, Mischief swears the inversion of the typical oath, i.e., to God or a saint. See Woolf, *English Mystery Plays*, pp. 136–37.

71        *Ande I wyll abyde*. I.e., Mischief responds not to the wishes of God but to those of the devil. In his frequent use of first person pronouns, Mischief "eschews the impersonal reference which so marks Mercy's speech and embraces the personal reference" (Beene, "Language Patterns in *Mankind*," p. 26). This informal and more intimate style of discourse — imitated by New Guise, Nought, and Nowadays — is fundamental to the successful seduction of Mankind as it produces a false sense of camaraderie and belonging.

71–72    Between these two lines a page containing approximately seventy lines is missing from the manuscript. In later lines, it is implied that Mercy had spoken about New Guise, Nought, and Nowadays (line 98). Beyond this, we can only speculate that the vices have intruded upon Mankind and are forcing him into games and dances against his will. Glynne Wickham conjectures that Nought is wearing a bearskin (*English Moral Interludes*, p. 5). Twycross notes that the minstrels present at the performance are playing the "bransle" with which an evening of dancing was started, according to Thoinot Arbeau's 1589 *Orchesographie* ("Theatricality," p. 79).

73        *ballys*. E suggests that "*ballys* may be the same word as *bales* in *M* 807, 'a rod or switch for flogging' (*MED baleis*)." Or perhaps it suggests whipping tops (i.e., spinning Mercy around). There is, however, no indication of violence in this case; perhaps they playfully prod Mercy into the dance, or perhaps they force Mercy into a game akin to the tossing of Mak in the blanket in the Towneley *Secunda Pastorum*. S reads *ballys* as "bellows," indicating the bagpipe, in which case the line would mean "Blow until your bagpipe bursts," or "Play until the dancer's belly bursts."

75        *Sent Tanne*. The cult of Saint Anne, the apocryphal mother of the Virgin Mary — and hence the grandmother of Jesus — flourished in the late fifteenth century (See Ashley and Sheingorn, *Interpreting Cultural Symbols*, p. 48). E cites *The Cely Papers*, "Sent Tannys mony" and "Sent Annys light" (pp. 186–87).

79        *Therfor ever beware of thi reporte*. L refers to this as an "uncharacteristically weak line," but then speculates that *reporte* is a pun meaning both talk and "musical sound."

81        *Have theratt then*. Nought finally joins in, but the witty pace is soon too much for him.

83        *Adam*. This was a name given to an old man, as if Nought were as old as the Adam of Genesis. Compare Shakespeare's Adam in *As You Like It*. Nought is made tired by all the vigorous activity.

85        *Yys, mary, I prey yow, for I love not this revelynge*. Sister Mary Philippa Coogan makes the case for Mercy speaking the line (*Interpretation of the Moral Play*,

*Mankind*, p. 507.) Though the line is appropriate for Mercy, it is also fitting for Nought, who has been worn out by his attempts to get Mercy to dance.

88    *play*. Though the manuscript reads *pray* there is better reason to think that Mercy would need to take off his outer garments to play than there is for him to pray.

97    *narow space*. The play appears to be performed amidst crowded conditions.

98–100    Presumably the dancing has ended and the vices now wish to speak with Mercy. Mercy continues to resist their games. In reaction, they claim that Mercy has called them (perhaps in the missing lines) and taken them away from their sleeping and eating, i.e., their sloth and gluttony. L (pp. 66–70) cites Anderson's *Drama and Imagery in English Medieval Churches* in noting that this sleeping and eating "may be meant to suggest the sins of sloth and gluttony."

101    *curtly*. Nowadays is asking Mercy to keep his speech as brief as possible, as he would like to get back to his eating. This is the only citation of the word in *MED*.

102    *Few wordys, few and well sett*. Mercy defends himself, saying that he will keep his address to them brief, and the words well-crafted. L notes that this line is "said ironically," as Mercy tends not to be brief.

103    *the new jett*. References to the new style or newfangledness are ubiquitous in later Middle English texts and usually carry an implication of wanton indulgence.

109    *lyke*. Compare the Towneley *Noah* play: "In fayth, and for youre long taryyng / Ye shal lik on the whyp" (lines 382–83).

110    *He was well occupyede that browte yow brethern*. L also reads this line as ironic, but, since we are not sure who brought the vices to this place, we can not be certain of Mercy's tone.

124    *Englysch Laten*. English that is made to seem formal by its Latinate sound, usually by additional syllables added to the end of the words, e.g., "denomination," "communication."

125–26    There are no rhymes for *brest* or *me*. As the following stanzas rhyme *aaabcccb*, it seems that there has been some confusion or omission in the copying of this stanza.

125–30    Furnivall and Pollard (*Macro Plays*, p. 5) and others present lines 125–28 and 130 in the footnotes, thus changing the line numbering.

126    *Pravo te*. New Guise begins a scene in which the vices both attempt to test Mercy's dexterity with Latin and to demonstrate their own proficiency, or at least their own sense of fun, with Latin. The ideological implications of this humorous exchange emerge from the fact that Mercy uses Latin not simply to restate ideas already made in English — as is frequently the case in *Piers Plowman*, for example — but as significant cornerstones to his argument throughout the play. E cites *Prauo* in *Ortus Vocabulorum* (c. 1500), in which it is defined as "to shrewe." The macronic verse, combining Latin and English, is common in this play as well as other morality plays and early Tudor drama.

| | |
|---|---|
| 129–38 | Manly cuts the whole stanza in his 1897 bowdlerized edition (*Specimens of the Pre-Shakesperean Drama*) as if to protect his more proper students from such foul language. |
| 133 | *opyn yowr sachell wyth Laten wordys*. Nowadays is setting Mercy to work to open up, in a sense, his "word-hoard" and set to work translating his couplet. Compare Free Will in *Hick Scorner*: "Nay, I have done, and you lade out Latin with scoops! But therewith can you clout me a pair of boots?" (lines 789–90). |
| 134 | *clerycall*. *OED* cites nothing for this word before 1592. See also line 579. |
| 139 | *twenti lyse*. Walker, *Medieval Drama*, p. 262, queries "20 li's, i.e., £20." Though this is reasonable from a paleographic point of view, the rhyme would be lost in the performance of the line. |
| 143–46 | This passage is clearly meant to be a lighthearted picture of the selling of indulgences, a biblically-based practice that, though profitable for the Church, eventually led to widespread abuse and criticism. Compare Chaucer's Pardoner. "Pope Pokett" is likely a reference to Prior John Poket of Barnwell Priory, as Jambeck and Lee first suggested ("Pope Pokett"); for accurate dates, see Salzman, *Victoria History of the County of Cambridge*, pp. 234–49. The reference to a local notable along with many others in the play contributes to its satirical edge. |
| 143 | *here ys a pardon bely-mett*. Nought has likely presumed a piece of paper to show that he has a pardon. E defines this as "to the measure of the belly, full and satisfying" and compares it to "bely-fyll" (line 639) and "fote-mett" (line 531). |
| 152 | *blyssyde Mary*. This should perhaps read "and blyssyde Mary," the sense being: "May God and Blessed Mary admit you to the brotherhood of the demonic friars." See also lines 325–26. |
| 153 | *demonycall frayry*. If Gail McMurray Gibson is correct in arguing that *Mankind* was written by a Benedictine monk at Bury St. Edmonds (*Theater of Devotion*), the phrase "demonycall frayry" may here be a pun on "Domincan friary." |
| 153–54 | A line is likely missing between these two lines, as there is nothing to rhyme with *eloquence* in line 150. |
| 154–55 | Compare *Mundus et Infans*, "come wynde and rayne, / God let hym neuer come here agayne!" (lines 491–92). |
| 160 | *jentyll Jaffrey*. The name clearly is meant as a light-handed insult. S suggests the name implies "a slow, listless man, a procrastinator" (p. 293). L cites John Heywood's *Proverbs*: "Nowe here is the doore, and there is the wey. And so (quoth he) farewell, gentill Geffrey." |
| 166 | *A best doth after hys naturall instytucyon*. Mercy's proof is that the vices are worse than beasts, since beasts act according to their own natural function while the vices go against nature in dishonoring Christ. |
| 173, 177 | L cites Matthew 12:36–37: "But I say onto you that every idle word that men shall speak, they shall render an account for it in the day of judgment. For by thy words thou shalt be justified; and by thy words thou shalt be condemned." |

180    *But such as thei have sowyn, such shall thei repe.* See Galatians 6:7: "Make no mistake
       about it; no one makes a fool of God! A man will reap only what he sows."

182    *The goode new gyse nowadays.* Mercy distinguishes here the good from the bad
       type of new fashion. He offers no description, however, of the good version and
       refers only to the "vycyouse gyse" or the bad type.

195    *Of a body and of a soull.* The dual nature of the human as the soul and the body
       was a common theme in medieval poetry, drama, sermons, and art. For
       example, in *W* Lucifer advises Mind, Will, and Understanding on the two
       natures: "Gode lowyt a clene sowll and a mery" (line 494) and "Yeue to yowr
       body þat ys nede, / Ande euer be mery; let reuell rowte!" (lines 504–05).

200    *Wher the goodewyff ys master, the goodeman may be sory.* In religious literature, the hier-
       archical relations between the body and soul were often described in the gendered
       metaphor of husband and wife: the proper order put the soul and the husband in
       the dominant positions over the body and the wife; when the body or wife ruled,
       trouble followed. Medieval popular culture exploited the humor in such upside-
       down gender roles; the Wakefield *Noah* play dramatizes Uxor Noah's obstreper-
       ousness, while Chaucer in his *Canterbury Tales* creates the irrepressible Wife of
       Bath to foreground the topic of marital *maistrye* in his narrative. E compares this
       line to the Scottish proverb, "It is a sour reek, where the good wife dings the
       good man" (*Oxford Dictionary of English Proverbs*, 1935 edition only, p. 228).

200–01 Because these lines appear in the margin, some early editors have omitted them
       or placed them in the footnotes. As this section is written in quatrains rhyming
       *abab*, these two lines are necessary to complete the quatrain.

204–05 As there is no rhyme for "dungehyll," a line between these two lines has likely
       been omitted accidentally.

229    Compare *MM*, "Now ar ye becum Goddys own knygth" (line 1952).

234    *chery tyme.* According to the *OED*, "cherry-fair" (here "cherry-time") was a symbol
       of the shortness of life and the fleeting nature of its pleasures. E compares
       Gower's *Confessio Amantis*, "Al is bot a cherie feire" (Prologue, line 454) and "as
       it were a cherie feste" (6.891) which suggest the transitoriness of gaity.

237    *Mesure ys tresure.* A common proverb in later Middle English indicating that hap-
       piness lies in the mean. Most directly at this moment he means that moderation
       in drink is to be observed.

241    *Yf a man have an hors and kepe hym not to hye.* This recommendation not to treat
       or feed a horse too well has, as S (p. 294) suggests, a parallel in Rolle's *A Treatise
       of Ghostly Battle*, in which Abstinence is the bridle to restrain the horse. Coogan,
       *Interpretation of the Moral Play, Mankind*, pp. 56–57, also cites *Speculum Sacerdotale*
       to the same effect.

248    *peson.* L notes that a peson is "a weighing instrument in the form of a staff with
       balls attached, whence a vulgar term for 'penis'" (p. 16). Bevington (*Medieval
       Drama*) and E suggest *pease* as a suitable gloss. Others have avoided the subject.
       To make the reading correct, L suggests that the line should read, "Ande

another ther I pysse [wyth] my peson." But "with" is not necessary. The idiom "piss my penis" is analgous to "shit my pants," "piss my pants," etc. We wouldn't say shit on/in my pants. L's "penis" makes better sense here than "pease."

252     *A goode horse shulde be gesunne.* New Guise, disagreeing with Mercy, claims, on practical grounds, that a good horse should be well fed. If Mercy kept the king's horses, he suggests, the king would have few horses. "Gesunne" is one of the most difficult words in the play. L's choice of *geason* means "scarce"; Furnivall and Pollard's choice of *gesumme* derives from the Old Norse *gørsemi*, which means plentiful (*Macro Plays*, p. 10). But L's reading as "scarce" makes the best sense.

262     *Do Lytyll.* E finds this used as a surname since 1204. See Reaney, *Dictionary of British Surnames*, p. 104.

270     *noblys.* A gold coin, worth ten shillings.

271     *Sent Qwyntyn.* Third-century Christian martyr who was tortured, beheaded, and thrown into the River Somme. In all cases, when the vices swear by any holy figure, it is ironic. See also lines 487 and 614.

274     *comyn tapster of Bury.* S cites an order at Lynn in 1465 to expel "eny common Tapster . . . whiche is knowen for a misgoverned woman" (p. 294). A common tapster would typically be a woman who operated a simple or cheap tavern. Compare the tapster who is not saved in the Chester *Harrowing of Hell* for "deceavinge manye a creature" (line 291) by not giving customers the amount of ale they had purchased.

286–92  *Se the grett pacyence of Job.* One of several references to Job, the Old Testament figure whose patience was severely tested by God. The scripture quoted in line 292 is Job 1:21. See also lines 228, 287–93, and 319–21. See further Stock, "Thematic and Structural Unity of *Mankind*."

287     *trieth.* L notes the *OED*: "To separate (metal) from the ore or dross by melting; to refine, purify by fire." Mankind, like Job, is to be tried like gold in the fire (Job 23:10).

301     *Tytivillus.* The fun-loving devil whose work it is to collect all the idle words, care-lessly-spoken prayers, and errors (especially those in Latin, spoken by priests); he stores them up in a huge satchel or wallet or writes them down on a scroll to use against the souls on Judgment Day. See Matthew 12:36: "But I say unto you, that every idle word that men shall speak they shall give account thereof on the Day of Judgment." See Introduction, pp. 7–8.

303     *ey.* Emended from "eyn" for the exact rhyme with "wey" (line 301) and as parallel to line 876.

308     *Do truly yowr labure and be never ydyll.* The contention between labor and idleness is the main idea of *OI*, which is perhaps the closest analogue to *Mankind*.

319     *remors.* E insists that it would be pronounced without the *r* sound, as with *mossel* (morsel) in *CP*, line 1171.

321       *Memento, homo, quod cinis es, et in cinerem reverteris.* The memorable text for Ash Wednesday services, derived from Job 34:15 "All flesh shall perish together, and man shall return into ashes" and Genesis 3:19 "dust thou art, and into dust thou shalt return." The *memento mori* (be mindful of your death) theme is prominent throughout the rest of the play.

322       *bagge of myn armys.* Though some have puzzled over this line, it seems apparent that Mankind is referring to an image of the cross on his chest. Whether the sign of the cross is, as S suggests, inscribed on paper and hung around Mankind's neck (p. 295) or shaped with a more permanent material is not clear. L notes that the "cross as badge of arms goes back to the Emperor Constantine's vision of it, when he heard the words: 'In this sign you shall conquer'" (p. 20). See also *MM*: "Here shall entyr þe thre Mariis arayyd as chast women, wyth sygnis of þe passyon pryntyd ypon þer brest" (line 992, s.d.).

325–26  *Ecce quam bonum et quam jocundum.* From Psalm 132:1 (Authorized King James Version 133:1). Mischief is trying to turn Mankind's argument against him and make Mankind feel like one of the friars, i.e., one of the order of the devils.

332       *Crystemes songe.* A "Christmas song" was a rowdy song that was part of seasonal revelry, according to S. E notes that "this is not 'a carol'" since it is not in stanzas (p. 220). It only has four lines that are presented as a travesty on instruction by lining. See Richard Rastall ("Sounds of Hell," pp. 120–31) on lining in psalmody. The leader/preacher sings the front line first which is then sung in a chorus by the congregation, here for a comic rather than pious effect since the words are obscene — a mouthful of turds, etc.

343       *Holyke.* This is clearly a profanation of the *sanctus* and the word *holy*, with scatological puns on *hole-ly, hole-like, hole-lick,* and *hole-leak.* E also suggests *hole-leek* may refer to a leek known as the holleke (p. 220).

348       *wyth bredynge.* Compare *Nature,* lines 525–30, "Let hym stand wyth a foule euyll . . . / Let hym stande on hys fete wyth bredyng."

373–75  Nought's scatological approach to farming is not unlike Mischief's approach to the metaphor of corn and chaff, both speakers being quite literal in their approaches. The notion that Mankind will "overblysse" his crops carries out the parody of the sacred that is prevalent throughout the play. E notes that according to the *OED* the earliest record of the use of "compasse" as "a mixture for fertilizing land" (i.e., compost) is 1587.

388       *Marryde I was for colde, but now am I warme.* Nought was cold, but the beating Mankind has given him has warmed him up.

390       *By cokkys body sakyrde.* L notes that swearing by Christ's body was akin to torturing him again. Compare *Nature,* i. 1174, "by cokkys precyouse body," and Chaucer's Pardoner's Tale, *Canterbury Tales* VI(C) 472–76.

398–99  *in spadibus. . . . hedybus.* In response to Mankind's biblical quotation, Nought uses nonsense Latin: *hedibus* (on the head) and *spadibus* (by the spade). In a sense, Nought is correct, as Mankind has been saved by his spade. Nought's mock-

Latin is part of a pseudo-academic motif that runs throughout this play and other comic morality plays such as *W* and *OI* and later humanist plays like *Wit and Science*.

426 ff.   In this scene Mischief shows the sort of compassion that Mercy has not shown to this point. L doubts Mischief's sincerity or the depth of his grief, a doubt well substantiated by the text. E.g. Mischief's "by him that me bought" in line 415 could refer to Satan or Titivillus more easily than Christ, given his perverse behavior and abuse of scripture. Compare his perversion (travesty) of "suffer the little children to come unto me" in lines 425–28, which produces the yowling babies he tries to silence with an apple, which he will give them "tomorrow." One wonders whether he has actually frightened (or perhaps just aggravated) some children in the audience.

435   Smart ("*Mankind* and the Mumming Plays") and others have compared this part of the action to the mumming plays.

440   *in nomine patris, choppe!* Nought combines the notion of beginning a prayer with "in the name of the father" with amputating his arm. In a sense, this is another example of the parody of the sacred, as Nought fears that Mischief will perform an unnecessary amputation with as little premeditation as he would begin a prayer.

446   *I hade a schreude recumbentibus but I fele no peyn.* To avoid Mischief's extreme remedies, New Guise and the others are pretending to be well.

449–50   Presumably they huddle to confer.

451   *How, how, a mynstrell!* They will use music to attract Titivillus, who will solve their problem.

452   *Walsyngham wystyll.* E and we follow S in concluding that the whistle was a souvenir sold to pilgrims at the shrine of Our Lady of Walsingham in Norfolk.

453   *flewte.* The rhyme would presumably be "flowte," but the playwright is not always insistent on exact rhymes, especially when he might be attempting a pun or another type of joke.

454   *I com wyth my leggys under me.* The first words uttered by Titivillus, thus beginning a new attempt to pervert Mankind. Titivillus, who foreshadows Shakespeare's Puck, Petruchio, and perhaps Falstaff, is the "star" of the show for all of his trickery, wild dress, and humor.

456   *si dedero.* The expectation is something in return, especially when Titivillus is the giver. Compare *CP* line 879. See Dean, *Medieval English Political Writings*, "Addresses of the Commons" (p. 164, note 23) for a satirical Latin song in couplets beginning "*Si dedero, decus accipiam flatumque favoris,*" with each couplet beginning "*Si dedero.*"

459 ff.   The vices take up a collection in order to pay for Titivillus' services. Most agree that this is in fact a collection for the players themselves. New Guise's singling out the *worshypfull soverence,* i.e., those who can afford to pay, is worth noting. In this pecuniary context, use of the phrase "gostly to owr purpos" is certainly

ironic. As Alan J. Fletcher notes ("Meaning," p. 302), the phrase is a sermon formula that signals the preacher's upcoming spiritual exegesis, asking the audience to be attentive to the spiritual truths which are found in the sermon. Used parodically here by New Guise, the phrase calls attention instead to the profane actions of the Worldlings.

460 *yowr neclygence.* A parody of "your reverence," which is the common idiom for addressing another respectfully.

461 *a hede that ys of grett omnipotens.* The big head was typical of characters in folk plays. The word *omnipotens* also parallels him with God, as we see elsewhere in the play.

462 *Kepe yowr tayll.* Nowadays tells the others to keep a careful account of the money they are about to collect; since they will need to pay Titivillus for his services, the Vices take a collection.

464–65 Titivillus does not like groats or tuppence; he prefers (more valuable) red royals, a coin worth ten shillings ("red" is synonymous with "gold"), first produced in 1465.

467 *goodeman of this house.* According to L, this refers to either "the master of this household" or "the host of this inn," depending on the acting location. They go on to imply that he is cursing them under his breath (for asking for money), but will not refuse (for fear of being shown up in public).

471 *I sey, New Gyse.* E construes this as "I speak in the new fashion," but it is clearly "I say [to you] New Guise [and] Nowadays: 'Are you well-moneyed?'" He is asking them if they have collected enough money to pay Titivillus for his services.

475 *Ego sum dominancium dominus.* Deuteronomy 10:17; Revelation 19:16. As the title refers to God and not to a devil, the use of the title here is ironic. Pilate in the Towneley *Processus Talentorum* (*Play of the Talents*) also refers to himself as *dominus dominorum* (line 10).

479 *I have no monay.* New Guise and the other vices, having supposedly collected money to pay Titivillus, have hidden the money and now claim to have none.

482 *felow.* E makes the case that the word should be *velan,* as it would rhyme with *jentyllman* (line 483) and assonate with (or make an imperfect rhyme with) *am* (line 484).

487 *Non nobis, domine, non nobis, by Sent Deny.* Psalm 113:9 (Authorized King James Version 115:1). As usual, the passage is quoted in an inappropriate context. As Titivillus is an inverted version of the true "dominus," the word "domine" is an appropriate address for a vice figure. Saint Denys, who became the patron saint of France, was bishop of Paris sent to convert Gaul in the Roman era. He was thrown to wild beasts, burnt at the stake, and then beheaded. His corpse is said to have risen from the dead and carried his severed head a great distance. In a sense, St. Denys would make a better patron for Nowadays, whose head was nearly amputated by Mischief, than for Nought.

488    *The Devll may daunce in my purse for ony peny.* Traditional proverb found in a variety of fifteenth- and sixteenth-century authors, including Hoccleve, Skelton, and Nashe. See Whiting, *Proverbs, Sentences, and Proverbial Phrases*, D191, and Tilley, *Dictionary of the Proverbs in England*, D233.

489    *clen as a byrdys ars.* Another traditional proverb. See Whiting, *Proverbs, Sentences, and Proverbial Phrases*, B317, and Tilley, *Dictionary of the Proverbs in England*, B391.

497    *the fyve vowellys.* S suggests that "v. wellys" (pp. 297–98) is a term synonymous with the five wounds of Christ. E thinks that "Nowadays may be varying this formula to refer to his cries of pain, 'A! e! i! o! u!'" The term might also be a malapropism.

498    *sytyca.* L notes the humor in this, as the sciatic nerve affects the leg and not the arm (p. 31).

505–15  All of the place-names and people listed by the vices here can be found in the East Midlands, with particular connections to the Cambridge area. See Introduction, p. 10. It is entirely possible, if the play were to be played in a variety of locations, that the players would use the names of those present in the audience to create the list in this section. If the names in the manuscript reflect that practice, then the audience for this performance at least would have been an impressive one. E notes that the place-names are discussed by Brandl, *Quellen des Weltlichen Dramas*, p. xxvi; by Furnivall and Pollard, *Macro Plays*, pp. xi–xii and 19; and by S pp. 48–55 and 306–08. In Cambridgeshire are Sawston, Hauxton, and Trumpington, a group of villages just south of Cambridge, and Fulbourn, Bottisham, and Swaffham, to the east of Cambridge in the direction of Bury (mentioned in line 274). East Walton, Gayton, Massingham, and another Swaffham are in Norfolk, a few miles to the east of Lynn. Swaffham and Soham in Cambridgeshire are mentioned in Skelton's "A Garlande or Chapelet of Laurell," line 1416. S cited documents for Huntingdons of Sawston in 1428, a John Thyrlowe of "Hawkeston" (also spelled "Hauston") in 1450, John and William Pychard of Trumpington (1450–89), William Baker of East Walton (d. 1491), Alexander Wood of Fulbourn (justice of the peace 1471), William Allington of Bottisham (justice of the peace 1457, speaker of the Commons in 1472, knighted in 1478, d. 1479), and Hamonds of Swaffham in Cambridgeshire and Swaffham in Norfolk. A John Fydde lived in 1450 at Waterbeach, near Cambridge. The rogues took care to avoid the two justices and "Hamonde of Soffeham," probably, as Bruce Dickens suggests, the William Hamond whose brass dated 6 Feb. 1481/2 was once at Swaffham Bulbeck, Cambs (Dickens et al., *Place-Names of Cumberland*). For the Huntingdon family see Teversham, *History of the Village of Sawston*, i. 52 *L*, 101–06. J. C. Wedgwood, *History of Parliament*, i. 9, records that William Allington, M.P., was exiled with Edward IV in September 1470, and is said to have been the king's standard-bearer at Barnet in April 1471 (p. 222).

512    *a noli me tangere.* John 20:17. The term is likely used here to note the character's arrogance or that he is a person best to avoid or "spare." In the *OED* the first use

of the phrase recorded as a description of a person is circa 1635. S cites two other instances before this date, in Gower and Lydgate (pp. 50–51).

516    *For drede of in manus tuas — qweke.* Nought's line works in a colloquial or oral fashion: for fear of being hung, i.e., like Christ on the Cross, whose last words were "*in manus tuas*" (Luke 23:46). In John 20:17, the reference is to the resurrected body of Christ, which Mary Magdalene is not to touch. He says that he will avoid Alyngton and Hamonde, perhaps because he has had legal troubles with them. The "qweke" is onomatopoetic, as in the sound of one's neck breaking on the gallows.

520    *neke-verse.* A man might escape hanging for his first offence if he could read a Latin verse (thus proving he was a cleric), usually Psalm 50:3: "*Miserere mei, Deus, secundum magnam misericordiam tuam; secundum multitudinem miserationum tuarum dele iniquitatem meam.*" For background on the practice of claiming benefit of clergy, see Gabel, *Benefit of Clergy in England*; also Firth, "Benefit of Clergy in the Time of Edward IV," where *Mankind* is discussed. This is first instance of "neke-verse" cited in *OED*. Compare *Hick Scorner*: "For we be clerks all and can our neck-verse" (line 266).

    *cheke.* Like *qweke* (line 516), this echoes the jolt of a hanging.

522    *I blysse yow wyth my lyfte honde.* The devil does everything in reverse of God, who blesses with the right hand, another parody of the sacred.

530    *my nett.* In his subtlety, the fiend is often portrayed ensnaring the idle with his net. See John Wyclif, *Select English Works*, 3.200, and Chaucer's Second Nun's Tale, *Canterbury Tales* VIII(G)8–13.

531    *I hope to have hys fote-mett.* Literally, Titivillus hopes to have the measure of Mankind's foot; in general, he hopes he can figure out how to bring Mankind to ruin.

537    *wyth drawke and wyth durnell.* These general terms for weeds that grow among grain are appropriate, as the subtext of this scene is the parable of the sower where weeds are sown along with the wheat, Matthew 13:24–30 and 36–43.

546    *I shall sow my corn at wynter and lett Gode werke!* L says that this "makes no sense since the setting already is winter, or very early spring" and opts for Bevington's suggested emendation of "at vyntur," meaning "at random" (p. 34). They have not allowed, however, for the fact that Mankind is slowly being worn down; when he discovers that the ground is too hard to till (thanks to Titivillus' board), Mankind decides that he can wait until winter to sow his seeds, probably of winter wheat. When winter comes, Mankind, who has quickly resigned himself to the fact that he will not get his crop planted, will "lett Gode werke."

549a    This stage direction is in the manuscript. Bevington places it after line 550 in his edition of the text (*Medieval Drama*, p. 923).

552    *Thys place I assyng as for my kyrke.* E notes that "the Lollards believed, according to the trial of William and Richard Sparke for heresy in 1457, that 'a prayer made in a field or other unconsecrated place is just as efficacious as if it were made in a church'" (p. 223).

566     *be Cryst*. The oath here is formulaic, and, as Titivillus works against Christ, ironic.

569–71    Unpolished silver has a powderlike hue to it: this fact along with the poor light will allow one to pass off silver brass as silver. Titivillus is likely taking this opportunity to show the audience one of his tricks or perhaps to take some coin or other valuable from one or more of them. Compare Skelton's *Magnificence* "my fancy was out of owl-flight" (line 671).

570     *powder of Parysch*. S suggests that this was an arsenic compound (p. 300).

582     *be on myle*. I.e., by the length of time it would take to walk a mile.

593     *The Devll ys dede*. Traditional saying: "the job is finished" or "My work is nearly done." Here Titivillus has nearly brought Mankind to sin or spiritual idleness.

607     *Whope who*. An untranslatable expression of someone waking with a start.

        *avows*. Not clear if he means *I avow* or *he (Titivillus) avows*; the former is grammatically incorrect, while the second is not possible, since Mankind does not even know that Titivillus had been there. The use of "avows" is likely to be colloquial for "I swear." See line 624.

611     *smattrynge*. Bevington (*Medieval Drama*, p. 925) glosses as "kissable?"; E, "?pretty." *MED* suggests "dirty," "foolish," or, as adj., "?attractive." "Kissable" seems in keeping with Mankind's eager mood. Certainly his thoughts are earthy as he recoils from his thwarted piety.

613     *overron*. As it is soon clear that New Guise has been involved in a series of crimes, it is generally assumed that he has just outrun the law.

        *Gode gyff hym evyll grace*. May God curse him, i.e., the man who was chasing New Guise.

614     *Sent Patrykes Wey*. New Guise, who enters with a noose around his neck, is indicating that he was near death when he saw St. Patrick's Way, or St. Patrick's Purgatory. St. Patrick's Way indicated a specific pit through which skeptical potential converts might glimpse Purgatory. Those who glimpsed this Purgatory, both in the time of St. Patrick and later when it became a popular destination for pilgrims, were supposedly converted; New Guise's morality, however, remains unchanged by the experience. E cites the Wright edition of *St. Patrick's Purgatory* and the Krapp edition of *The Legend of St. Patrick's Purgatory*.

616     *ecce signum*. Presumably, he is holding the noose (the sign) in his hands as he piously would have us "behold the proof." The Latin phrase parodies Christ's showing of His wounds to the disciples as evidence of His resurrection and becomes a favorite comic trope in Renaissance drama. Compare Marlowe's *Doctor Faustus* 3.2.2 (Robin); Shakespeare's *I Henry IV* 2.4.187 (Falstaff), and *Taming of the Shrew* 1.3.227 (Sonder). See Rainer Pineas on the vice figure's self-condemnation in *Mankind* ("English Morality Play," pp. 162–65).

617     *a nere rune*. First instance in *OED* of the noun *run*.

618     *Beware.* A bit of dark humor, as her warning to her husband comes at the same moment that she takes off his head. As we learn in line 644, Mischief has been dallying with the woman, who was also the wife of the jailer.

619     *Mischief ys a convicte.* Mischief is a convict, i.e., imprisoned rather than hanged, because he was able to recite the "neck verse." See also line 520n.

621     *he wyll hange such a lyghly man.* According to the *MED,* "lyghly" ("handsome/ trustworthy/honest, excellent") is a rare word in Middle English. Compare *W:* "Me semyt myselff most lyghly ay" (line 554), and *MM:* "So it is most lylly for to be!" (line 1265).

628     *Sent Audrys holy bende.* New Guise, who is wearing a broken noose around his neck, tells the credulous Mankind that he wears the saint's emblem to help cure his ringworm. Silk lace neckbands were purchased at the shrine of St. Audrey in Ely Cathedral and worn by women in the later Middle Ages and Renaissance to commemorate the revered saint who died of a tumor on her neck, a tumor which she considered appropriate payment for her own vanity of wearing beautiful necklaces in her youth. Later referred to as *tawdry lace.*

630     *runnynge ryngeworme.* New Guise uses the noose marks to make a visual pun on his "lytyll dyshes."

632     *I have laburryde all this nyght; wen shall we go dyn.* This seems to be an ironic version of Luke 5:5, when Christ calls his disciples and Simon answers "Master, we have been hard at it all night long and have caught nothing."

633     *A chyrche her besyde shall pay for ale, brede, and wyn.* Nowadays has robbed a church: he has stolen either church properties, including perhaps the Eucharist and sacramental wine, or cash and other items that will afford him enough money for ale, bread, and wine.

638     *Here cummyth a man of armys.* A joke that he has the remnants of shackles on his arms, playing perhaps on the fact that a man of arms placed them there. Compare Youth's line "thou diddest enough there / For to be made knight of the collar" in *Youth* (lines 269–70).

641     *scoryde a peyr of fetters.* A double meaning for *scoryde:* to *scour* or wear clean, i.e., through his efforts to escape, and *scored,* i.e., to win by stealing, though this use is not recorded until much later.

647     *I brought awey wyth me both dysch and dublere.* Mischief's theft of food items from the jailer, combined with Nowadays' stolen items from a church, will serve to parody the Last Supper, or at least the sacrament of Eucharist, as the vices sit down to eat. See Pineas, "English Morality Play," pp. 159–64.

649     *the new chesance.* The "new chesance" comes through corruption and deceit. Compare the N-Town "Jerusalem Conspiracy": "And yf mony lakke, this is the newe chevesauns" (line 103). Chaucer's Merchant in the *Canterbury Tales* (Prologue I[A] 282) keeps up his prosperous appearance through ostentatious "chevyssaunce," or monetary dealings.

661     *Why stonde ye so styll?* Either Mankind has become frozen in his despair or, as L suggests, the line is spoken sarcastically about Mankind, who is "trembling like a leaf."

664     *sett a corte.* Rather than simply registering Mankind as one of his own, Mischief holds court to decide if he is worthy. The following scene, usually referred to as "the court of Mischief" or "the court of misrule," is another case of the parody of the sacred in which the normal order of things, including court proceedings, is turned upside down. This scene both parallels the Last Judgment scenes in the cycle plays and anticipates the Boar's Head Tavern trial scene in Shakespeare's *1 Henry IV*, II.iv., in which Prince Hal (not unlike Mankind in many ways) is put on trial by his would-be father Falstaff.

667     *Oyyt! Oyyt! Oyet! Macro Plays*, ed. Bevington, p. 289: *O y yt, Oy ʒyt, Oyet*. Though the spellings are seemingly unusual here, there seems to be no consistency in other texts. An imperfect pronunciation would be appropriate and perhaps comic here.

668     *sen.* The playwright uses a shortened form of *send* to rhyme with *women* and *men*. E notes that "tenants were bound either to attend the manor court or to send excuses ('essoins')" (p. 225).

671     *syde gown.* This scene includes an ongoing visual gag in which Mankind's stately garment is step-by-step reduced to a ridiculous remnant of its original self. New Guise's attempt to tailor a "fresch jakett" (line 676) turns out to be, according to Nowadays, "not be worth a ferthynge" (line 695). Nought says he will "mende yt" and returns with a "joly jakett" (line 718), which is cause for much laughter. It is also an image of topical interest: S cites a 1463 statute that prohibited any man from wearing a "gown, jacket, or coat, unless it be of such length that the same may cover his privy members and buttocks" (pp. 304–05).

687–90  *Carici tenta generalis. . . Anno regni regitalis / Edwardi nullateni.* This is a parody of the opening lines of a court session or court record. Edward the Nothing is likely an allusion to the fact that, after Edward IV's deposition in 1470, there is a short period in which England had no monarch.

687     *Carici tenta generalis.* It should read "*Curia tenta generalis*" (The general court having been held). Mischief's Latin is weak.

691     *On yestern day in Feverere — the yere passyth fully.* Mischief considers March 1 to be the first day of the year.

692     *Tulli.* Common name for Marcus Tullius Cicero in the Middle Ages. If the reference is to Nought, it is an ironic one, since Cicero, not Nought, was the paradigm of models and Latin rhetoric.

705–06  "*I wyll," sey ye. I wyll, ser.* Though this is, in general, a court scene, it may also be a parody of baptism or other sacraments, with Mankind making vows to carry out the articles of his new faith. See also line 718n.

712     *matins, owres, and prime.* Three of the seven canonical hours or offices he would be expected to attend under Mercy's direction. The seven offices were, from morning to evening: matins, prime, terce, sext, none, vespers, and compline.

714      *da pacem*. Ironically, the dagger, which Mischief gives the unusual nickname of "Give Peace," would put his victims to rest.

718      Mankind's donning of the "joly jakett" is not unlike the catechumen's vesting of the baptismal gown. Compare Ydelnes' taking of the "clothe of clennes" in *OI* (line 812). See also lines 705–06n.

719      *jake of fence*. As the jesters keep shortening Mankind's coat they are both robbing him and effeminizing him. See *MED* "jakke" n.(2)c *jacke of fence*, "a short tunic worn by women."

720      *Hay, doog, hay!* New Guise encourages Mankind for his new fashion, perhaps as a hunter would stir up his dogs.

724      *I beschrew the last shall com to hys hom*. As in modern children's games, the one who comes in last is cursed. Compare *Hick Scorner*, "Beshrew him for me that is last out of this place!" (line 545).

729      *Stow, statt, stow!* E (p. 225) glosses as "Ho, woman, ho!" and compares N-Town's "Woman Taken in Adultery," 24.125: "Stow [stop] that harlot," and 145: "Come forth thu stotte [slut]." The vices are beginning to engage in a sort of children's game here in which they confound Mercy. Soon it turns to football. "Stow" is perhaps a call to hounds; "statt" may be a word referring to a woman, though this is not clear from the context.

732      *ostlere, hostlere! Lende us a football*. The fact that they are asking the innkeeper for a football has led most readers to believe that *Mankind* was meant to be performed at Shrovetide, the three days preceding Ash Wednesday, which was a time of carnival and games.

742      *Man onkynde*. A pun on the name Mankind.

743      *To dyscharge thin orygynall offence*. Mercy is drawing a distinction between what the world, along with its vices, can do to relieve humans of original sin, i.e., nothing, and what "Godys own welbelovyde son" has done. The theme of original sin is important in *W* as well, e.g., lines 103–32.

750      *In trust ys treson*. A common proverb in the later Middle Ages. See Whiting, *Proverbs, Sentences, and Proverbial Phrases*, T492.

753–55      The versifier is unidentified, but S (p. 302) quotes similar verses in Latin and English in Gower, *Confessio Amantis*, 5.vii (3:142): "*cvncta creatura, deus et qui cuncta creaiut, / Dampnant ingrati dicta que facta viri*" [Every creature, God, and all that he created, condemn the words and deeds of an ungratful man]. S goes on to note Gower's amplication of the idea in *Confessio Amantis* 5.4917–22 (3:143): "The bokes speken of this vice, / And telle hou God of His justice, / Be weie of kinde and ek nature / And every lifissh creature, / The lawe also, who that it kan, / Thei dampnen an unkinde man." E compares to Lydgate, *Minor Poems*, ii. 583, "Lawe and nature pleynyn on folke vnkynde" (p. 226). See Galloway, "Making of a Social Ethic in Late-Medieval England."

759      *Equyté to be leyde onparty and Mercy to prevayll*. Mercy echoes the position of Mercy and Justice in the familiar debate of the Four Daughters of God that is given prominence in N-Town's "Parliament of Heaven," lines 53–188; *CP* lines 3129–3560; and nondramatic texts such as *Cursor Mundi*, lines 9517–52; Grosseteste's *Chateau d'Amour*; *The Court of Sapience*; and Langland's *Piers Plowman* B.18.

771      *ubi es?* L notes that "Mercy's distressed search for Mankind recalls the parable of the good shepherd who searches for the lost sheep until it is found (Luke 15:3–7)" (p. 48).

773      *sowpe out yowr messe*. Mercy is repeating the phrase "*ubi es*" ("where are you"), so it begins to sound like "supie." Mischief's reply is that if Mercy wishes to use such terms, he should do so moderately (in measure).

776–77   The pun of seeking and sighing is typical of the language of the Worldlings in the play.

780–81   *a cape corpus . . . non est inventus*. Nowadays is telling Mercy that if he would like to see Mankind he must have a *capias*, or writ of arrest; if he does not have a capias the sheriff will reply that Mankind is not found.

782      *My bolte ys schett*. Nowadays has finished his defecatory labors. There is perhaps here an appropriate pun on *schett*. Compare "A fool's bolt is soon shot" (Smith and Wilson, *Oxford Dictionary of English Proverbs*, p. 216).

786      *My fote ys fowly overschett*. Nought has noted in four successive assertions that there has been an "accident," but it is not clear who (other than his bowels) has caused the accident.

787      *Cum forth, Nought, behynde*. Mischief tells the three vices to come forward, but, realizing that Nought's foot does not smell pleasant, directs him to stand back. There may be a further pun on "behynde" as well.

790      *A flyes weyng*. Compare the Towneley *Buffeting Play* (*Colophizacio*): "he settys not a fle wyng / bi sir cesar full euen" (lines 137–38).

796      *Sent Gabryellys modyr save the clothes of thi schon*. This is high praise for New Guise's plan to drive Mankind to despair by telling him that Mercy has been hanged for stealing a mare: for devising such a plan Saint Gabriel's own mother should preserve the fabric of his beshitten shoes.

802      *Wyth a tre also that I have gett*. I.e., they have prepared a makeshift gallows.

804      *Do as I do; this ys thi new gyse*. New Guise shows Mankind how to use the noose, the latest thing in quick executions, prompting Mercy finally to support his words with action as he reenters with a whip and begins to chase Mischief.

807      *bales*. According to Mark Chambers, the bale(y)s is best understood as a specific type of whip used as a tool of penitence in either a sacrificial or a disciplinary method ("Weapons of Conversion," pp. 1–2). Compare to *MM* lines 735–39.

808      *Qweke, qweke, qweke!* Choking sounds. See line 520n.

809      Saint David's day was celebrated liturgically on March 1.

812     *vytall spryt.* According to medieval physiology, the three spirits which controlled the processes of life were the natural (located in the liver), the vital (in the heart), and the animal (in the brain) (L, p. 51).

813–14     Mankind is embarrassed for Mercy to see him in his present state, so "bestyally dysposyde."

817–18     Compare with *W*: "*Fili, prebe michi cor tuum.* / I aske not ellys of all þi substance. / Thy clene hert, þi meke obeysance, / Yeue me þat and I am contente" (lines 79–82).

826     *hec est mutacio dextre Excelsi; vertit impios et non sunt.* Psalm 76:11 (Authorized King James Version 77:10) and Proverbs 12:7. Note that it is not quite either one: Psalm 76:11 "And I said, Now have I begun: this is the change of the right hand of the most High" and Proverbs 12:7 "Turn the wicked, and they shall not be: but the house of the just shall stand firm."

830     *Miserere mei.* The opening of Psalms 50, 55, 56 (Authorized King James Version 51, 56, 57). This is the "neke-verse" noted in line 520.

834     *Nolo mortem peccatoris, inquit.* Abbreviated from Ezechiel 33:11, which actually reads: "*Nolo mortem impii, sed ut convertatur impius a via sua, et vivat.*"

839–42     Mercy explains that at the Last Judgment Justice, Equity, and Truth will all try to condemn Mankind, but Mercy will win the debate and save Mankind's soul. Three of the four daughters of God (Justice, Truth, and Mercy) are named; Peace is the fourth. See Psalm 84:11 (Authorized King James Version 85:10): "Mercy and truth have met each other; justice and peace have kissed." See line 759n. The fact that in *Mankind* Truth and Mercy are male is troubling to L (p. 53). The same gender conflation is present in the figure of Wisdom in *W*.

845     *Synne not in hope of mercy.* Compare Ecclesiasticus 5:6: "And say not: The mercy of the Lord is great, he will have mercy on the multitude of my sins."

846     *To truste overmoche in a prince yt ys not expedient.* Compare Psalm 145:2 (Authorized King James Version 146:3): "Put not your trust in princes."

862     *usque ad minimum quadrantem.* Compare Matthew 5:26, "*Amen dico tibi non exies inde donec reddas novissimum quadrantem*": "Amen I say to thee, thou shalt not go out from thence till thou repay the last farthing." "The language echoes Matthew 5:26, and the theme recalls the struggle of Everyman to clear his book of accounts" (L, p. 54).

863     *Aske mercy and have.* Compare Matthew 7:7: "Ask, and it shall be given you: seek, and you shall find: knock, and it shall be opened to you" and N-Town's "Woman Taken in Adultery": "Haske thu mercy and thu shalt have" (line 24).

866     *Ecce nunc tempus acceptabile, ecce nunc dies salutis.* 2 Corinthians 6:2: "For he saith: In an accepted time have I heard thee and in the day of salvation have I helped thee. Behold, now is the acceptable time: behold, now is the day of salvation." L also cites Isaiah 49:8. Coogan notes that this is the epistle reading on the first

Sunday of Lent (*Interpretation of the Moral Play, Mankind*, p. 11). E notes that it is also included in Matins on Ash Wednesday.

868    Late medieval theological orthodoxy emphasized that one cannot *earn* heaven by virtuous deeds; salvation is a gift of a merciful God. However, pastoral teaching emphasized the need to repent of one's sins well before death and facing judgment, since mercy will not be available at that time.

883–88    *thre adversaryis.* The notion of the three enemies of mankind — the World, the Flesh, and the Devil — is ubiquitous in late Middle English literature. Compare *OI*: "Euery man hath enmyes thre, / þe Deuel, þe World, and his owen Flessh" (lines 374–75) and *W*: "Ye haue thre enmyes; of hem be ware: / The Worlde, þe Flesche, and þe Fende" (lines 293–94).

884    *the Flesch and the Fell.* While flesh refers more to the meat, the fell refers to the skin itself.

912    *per suam misericordiam.* "Through his mercy": a phrase often found in prayers and commentaries but never as a complete phrase in the Bible. The phrase "*secundum suam misericordiam*" is found in Titus 5:2, 1 Peter 1:3, and Ecclesiasticus 50:24.

913    *pleyferys.* E notes that "Henry Bradley, in Furnivall, p. 188a, pointed out that this should be *pleyferys* and compared 'aequales angelis' in Luke xx. 36. Compare *Peter Idley's Instructions to His Son*, p. 542, 'In heuene who shal be my playefeeris'" (p. 227).

**ABBREVIATIONS: B**: Bevington, *Medieval Drama*; **B₂**: *Macro Plays*, ed. Bevington; **C**: Colde-wey; **E**: Eccles; **F**: Farmer; **FP**: Furnivall and Pollard; **L**: Lester; **M**: Manly; **MS**: Washington, Folger Shakespeare Library 5031; **s.d.**: stage direction; **WA**: Walker.

F and L are modernized editions of the text and are only included in the following notes when there is significant variation in the readings or when they offer a noteworthy point of comparison. B and C are partially modernized editions; variations are noted here when they are more than simple modernizations or when they offer a noteworthy point of comparison.

| | |
|---|---|
| 3 | *dysobedyenc*. So E. M, FP, C: *dysobedyenc[e]*. WA: *dysobedyence*. B: *disobedienc[e]*. |
| 7 | *hade*. M: emends to *late* from *lade*. F, C: *have*. |
| 9 | *Yt*. FP: *þat*. M, F: *That*. |
| 21 | *The*. MS: ~~To~~ *þe*. |
| 22 | *medyacyon*. So M, E, WA, C. MS, FP: *medytacyon*. B: *mediacion*. |
| | *habundante*. M: emends to this from *hadundance*. B: *habunda[u]nte*. F: *abundant*. |
| 23 | *neclygence*. M: *ne[g]lygence*. |
| 26 | *be*. WA omits. |
| 27 | *avaunte*. So B, E, C, WA. MS: *a vaunce*. M, FP: *a-vaunte*. F, L: *avaunt*. |
| 31 | *Beholde*. MS: *Be holde*. M, FP: *Be-holde*. |
| | *yowr*. MS: *w yowr*. M: *yower*. FP: *yowur*. |
| 32 | *Se*. C: *se[e]*. |
| 33 | *certyfye*. So M, FP, E, C, WA. MS: *crertyfye*. B: *certifye*. F, L: *certify*. |
| before 35 | In the top margin of this folio a line has been scratched out and is close to illegible. According to B₂, it may read: *A And yf ther be any man or womans*. |
| 37 | *londe*. M: *lande*. |
| 40 | *vemynousse*. MS: the *sse* is blurred. M: *[the] venymouse*. C: *venymousse*. B: *venimousse*. |
| 42 | *ther*. So C. MS: *þe*. E, FP: *þer*. F, L: *there*. B: *the[r]*. WA: *þe[r]*. M: *ther*. |
| | *streyt*. So C. MS, F, FP: *strerat*, FP queries *strait* or *strict*. M: emends to *streat* from *sterat*. B, L: *strait*. |
| 45 | *calcacyon*. So FP, WA, C. M: *calc[ul]acyon*. F: *calculation*. B: *calc[ul]acion*. |
| 48 | *prey*. So E, WA. FP: *prey [yow]*. F: *pray [you]*. L: *pray you*. B: *prey [you]*. |
| 49 | *Mysse-masche, dryff-draff*. So WA, C. MS: *dryff draff mysse mache*. F: *Driff, draff! mish, mash!* M, FP: *Dryff-draff, mysse-masche*. L: *Mish-mash, driff draff*. B: *Missse-masche, driff-draff*. |
| 52 | *Onschett*. MS, B, FP: *On-schett*. M: *On-shett*. |
| 55 | *feryde*. M: emends to *fyryde* from *feryrde*. F, L: *fired*. |

| | |
|---|---|
| 60 | *reliqua*. M: *reliquid*. FP, F: *reliqu[i]d*. |
| 61 | *provente*. M, FP, F: *produce*. |
| 62 | *forcolde*. MS: *for colde*. M, FP, F, B: *for-colde*. |
| 64 | *Avoyde*. MS: *A voyde*. M, FP: *A-voyde*. |
| 66 | *nor*. MS: the *no* is blotted. M: emends to this from *for*. |
| 67 | *may*. MS: the *y* is blotted. |
| 68 | *on*. MS: the *on* is blotted. |
| 70 | *not*. MS: this word is added above *go*. |
| | *devyllys name*. MS: *deuyllys ~~man~~ name*. WA: *Devllys name*. B: *dev[i]llys name*. |
| 71 | *abyde*. MS: *a byde*. M: *a-byde*. |
| 71a | MERCY. The speaker's part is added at the bottom of folio 122v; a leaf of the manuscript is apparently missing after this. |
| 72 | NEW GYSE. MS: though no name is recorded here, New Guise is likely speaking. FP, F, E, B, L, C, WA all concur. M: *Mercy*. |
| 73 | *ballys*. M: emends to *bowys* from *bollys*. F: *bales*. L: *baleys*. |
| 74 | *neke*. M: emends to this from *reke*. |
| 75 | *no*. M: emends to this from *us*. |
| 76 | *Leppe*. M: emends to this from *Leffe*. F, L: *Leap*. |
| | *about*. MS: *a bout*. M, FP: *a-bout*. |
| | *wyght*. F: *white*. |
| 77 | *wyll*. F, L: *while*. B: *w[h]ill*. C: *w[h]yll*. |
| 78 | *schew*. M, F, L: *show*. FP: *schow*. |
| 79 | NOWADAYS. MS: NOW~~ADY~~ A DAYS. |
| | *beware*. MS, WA, C: *be ware*. FP: *be-ware*. |
| 80 | *beschrew*. MS: *be schrew*. M, FP: *be-shrew*. |
| | *Her*. B: *Her[e]*. |
| 81 | *theratt*. MS, FP: *þer att*. WA: *þeratt*. M: *ther at*. |
| | *then*. MS, E, WA: *þen*. FP: *þem*, queries *þen*. M, F: *them*. B, L, C: *then*. |
| 81, s.d. | *daunce*. So M, FP, E, C. MS: *daunc*. B, WA: *daunc[e]*. F, L: *dance*. |
| 82 | *reull*. M, FP: *reuell*. B: *rev[e]ll*. C: *revll*. L: *revel*. |
| 83 | *goode*. MS: *gode*, with the additional *o* added above the rest of the word. |
| 84 | *thi*. MS, E, WA: *þi*. M: *thin*. |
| 86 | *Cum*. M: *Euer*. |
| 88 | *Anon*. MS: *A non*. M, FP: *A-non*. |
| | *play*. So E, B, C, WA. MS, M, FP, F, L: *pray*. |
| 90 | *daunce*. M: emends to this from *dauunce*. |
| 92 | *avaunce*. MS: *a vaunce*. M, FP: *a-vaunce*. |
| 96 | *tracyed*. MS, B: *tracyde*. |
| | *to fell*. So M, suggests *~~fylde~~ fell*. MS: *~~fylde~~ fell*. FP: *fylde fell*. B, C: *to[o] fell*. |
| 97 | *tell yt ys*. So E, WA. M, FP: *tell [yow] yt ys*. F, B: *tell [you] it is*. L: *tell, it is*. C: *tell yow [it] ys*. |
| 99 | *hade*. M: *haue ʒe*. FP: *had ʒe*. F: *have ye*. B: *hade [ye]*. L: *have*. |
| 100 | *And*. So E, L, C. MS: *A*. M, FP, WA, F, B: *A[nd]*. |
| | *cuppe*. So M, E, B, C, WA. MS: *cuppe redy*. F, L: *cup*. FP: retains *redy*. |
| 106 | *synfull*. So E, WA, C. MS, FP: *sympull*. M: *synnfull*. F: *simple*. B: *simpull*. |
| 107 | *not*. M, F, B: *no[ugh]t*. L: *nought*. |
| | *ageyn*. MS: *a geyn*. FP: *a-geyn*. |

|         | |
|---------|---|
|         | *nowadays.* MS: *now a days.* M, FP, F: *Now-a-days.* |
| 108     | *schrewys.* So E, C. MS: *schewys.* M, FP, WA, B: *sch[r]ewys.* F: *sh[r]ews.* L: *shrews.* |
| 109     | *lyke.* MS: k̶ *lyke.* |
|         | *boffett.* MS, FP, WA, C, B: *bofett.* F, L: *buffet.* |
| 110     | *brethern.* M: *hether.* F: *hither.* B, C, L: *brether.* |
| 111     | *togethere.* MS: *to gethere.* M, FP: *to-gether.* |
| 113     | *Lo.* M: *So.* |
| 115     | *NOWADAYS.* MS: this is not written as a speech tag. |
|         | *NOUGHT.* MS: this is not written as a speech tag. |
| 117     | *betray.* MS: *be tray.* M, FP: *be-tray.* |
|         | *men.* MS: A̶ m̶a̶n̶ *men.* |
| 118     | *Betray.* MS: *Be tray.* M, FP: *Be-tray.* |
| 122     | *by.* MS: a̶n̶d̶ m̶y̶, *by* added above line. M, FP: *& my.* F, L: *and my.* |
| 123     | *favour.* MS, E: *fauour.* M: emends to *fors* from *fans.* FP: *faus.* F: *force.* |
| 125–26  | MS: lines copied incorrectly as neither has a corresponding rhyme. |
| 125–28  | MS: lines added to the right of the text. M and FP place these lines in a footnote so line numbers are different from those of this edition from this point on. F does not include these lines. |
| 126     | *onto.* MS: *on to.* FP: *on-to.* L: *unto.* |
| 127     | *stale.* M: *stall.* L: *stole.* |
| 128     | B attributes this line to Nowa[days]. |
| 129     | *NOWADAYS.* MS: *Now A* added in the left margin. |
|         | *worschyppull.* M: *worschypfull.* FP: *worschypp[f]ull.* B: *worshipp[f]ull.* |
| 130     | MS: the line itself appears in the right margin above 125; this edition follows E and B in the line ordering. M, FP, F consider it a note and omit. |
| 133     | *Laten.* M: *Lat[en].* |
| 135     | *Rachell.* M: *Rackell.* F: *Rachel.* |
| 140     | *thee.* C: *the[e].* MS, E: *þe.* M: *the.* FP: *þee.* WA: *þe[e].* |
| 141     | *that.* M: emends to this from *late.* MS, E, FP, WA: *þat.* |
| 142     | *Osculare fundamentum.* MS: written in the right margin. |
| 143     | *bely-mett.* MS: *bely mett.* M: emends to *bely mett* from *bely melt.* F: *by limit.* |
| 145     | *sockett.* MS, E, M, FP, WA, C, B: *sokett.* |
| 147     | *ydyll.* M: emends to this from *yeyll.* |
| 149     | *hens.* M: emends to this from *haue.* |
| 151     | MS: *In the name of God amen* is written in the right margin next to this line in a different hand. |
| 153–54  | MS: as there is no line to rhyme with *eloquence* (line 150), it appears that a line is missing between these lines (M, E agree). |
| 154     | *NOWADAYS.* MS: *nowad,* with *novadeis* written in the right margin. Also true of lines 336, 338, 340, 342, 442, 462, 473, 483, 640, 683, 694, and 795. |
|         | *Cum.* M: *Euer.* |
| 155     | *ageyn.* MS: *a geyn.* M, FP: *a-geyn.* |
| 159     | *her.* C: *her[e].* |
| 161, s.d. | *simul.* M omits. FP: *silentio.* |
|         | *Cantent.* MS: this is written in another hand. M, FP omit. F: *sil.* |
| 167     | *behavour.* MS: *be hauour.* M, FP: *be-hauour.* |
| 169     | *her.* M, B: *[t]her.* F, L: *their.* |

| | |
|---|---|
| 171 | *Beware.* MS, M, FP, WA, C: *Be ware.* |
| 172 | *befor.* MS: *be for.* M, FP: *be-for.* |
| 173 | *ydyll.* M: emends to this from *yeyll.* |
| | *we.* M: *ws.* |
| 174 | *ease.* M: *ca[u]se.* |
| | *thei.* MS, E, FP, WA: *þei.* M: *the[i].* |
| 177 | *onto.* MS: *on to.* M, FP: *on-to.* F, L: *unto.* |
| 178 | *begyn.* MS: *be gyn.* M, FP: *be-gyn.* |
| | *sore.* M, FP: *sor.* |
| 185 | *that.* MS, E, FP, WA: *þat* both times. M: emends from *yt* both times. |
| 186 | *cley.* M: emends to *gler* from *cler,* queries *cley.* |
| 189 | *onto.* MS: *on to.* M, FP: *on-to.* F, L: *unto.* |
| 192 | *pervercyonatt.* M: *pervertonnat.* FP, B: *pervercionatt.* |
| 193 | *them.* MS, E, WA: *þem.* FP: *þes.* F: *these.* M: *thes.* |
| 196 | *them.* MS, E, WA: *þem.* M, F: *the.* FP: *þe.* |
| 197 | *subjecte.* So E, B, C, WA. MS: *subiecte.* M: emends to *soiette* from *seietle.* FP: *s[u]biecte.* F: *s[u]bject.* |
| 200 | *goodewyff.* MS: *goode wyff.* M, B: *goode-wyff.* |
| | *goodeman.* MS: *goode man.* M: *goode-man.* |
| 201 | *remembrance.* M: *remembrence.* |
| 201–02 | MS: these lines are added in the right margin with the end of line 201 written above the rest of the line. M, FP, and F consider them notes and omit. E places them here. B, L, C, and WA follow E. |
| 202–03 | MS: as there is no line to rhyme with *dungehyll* (line 204), it appears that a line is missing between these lines. |
| 202 | *O thou.* MS: *O þu.* M: *& in.* FP: *O In.* B: *O th[o]u.* |
| 203 | *Alasse.* MS: *A lasse.* FP: *A-lasse.* |
| 204 | *dungehyll.* MS: *dunge hyll.* FP: *dunge-hyll.* |
| 206 | *trodyn.* MS: ~~*Dred*~~ *trodyn.* |
| 207 | *asay.* MS: *a say.* M, F, L: *assay.* FP: *a-say.* |
| 210 | *wysdam.* M: *wysdaum.* |
| 216 | *synfull.* So E, C, WA. MS, FP: *sympull.* M: *synnfull.* |
| 220 | *To.* MS: *Ɨ To.* |
| 221 | *O.* C omits. |
| | *vertu.* MS: this is added above *ye are.* M: *vertue.* |
| 224 | *hat.* M, B, C: *hat[h].* F, L: *hath.* |
| 225 | *wordys.* M: *workes.* FP: *workis.* F: *works.* |
| 227 | *betwyx.* MS: *be twyx.* |
| 228 | *milicia.* So FP, E. MS: *nnilicia.* B, L: *militia.* |
| 230 | *ageyn.* MS: *a geyn.* FP: *a-geyn.* |
| | *yowr.* FP: *yowur.* M: *yower.* |
| 231 | *Yf.* M, F: *If.* |
| 232 | *yow.* F: *you[r].* |
| 237–38 | MS: these are recorded as one line that extends into the right margin. |
| 240 | *anon.* MS: *a non.* M, FP: *a-non.* |
| 248 | *another.* MS: *a noþer.* M: *a-nother.* FP: *a-noþer.* WA: *anoþer.* |
| | *pysse.* M: emends to this from *pyose.* |

| | |
|---|---|
| 249 | *to-banne.* MS: *to banne.* M: *to-sane,* queries *to-lam.* FP, F: *to-samne.* |
| 251 | *palfrey-man.* M: *palfrey-man,* queries *mare.* E, WA, C: *palfreyman.* |
| 252 | *horse.* M: *horses.* |
| | *gesunne.* So E, C. MS, FP, F, WA: *gesumme.* B: *gesunne.* M: emends to *geson* from *gesumma.* L: *geason.* |
| 255 | *Hym.* MS: ~~Us~~ *hym.* |
| 257 | *son.* FP: *sone.* F, L: *soon.* B: *son[e].* C: *so[o]n.* |
| 261 | *anon.* MS: *a non.* M: *a-non.* |
| 264 | MS: *Novad* is written in the right margin, though Nowadays' part began at line 261. |
| | *Mo then.* MS, E, FP, WA: *Mo þen.* M: *Me thynk.* |
| 265 | *leve.* M emends to *leue* from *leuer.* F: *liever.* |
| 266 | *When.* M: *To [t]hem.* FP: *to hem.* F: *To them.* |
| 268 | *Because.* MS: *Be cause.* M, FP: *Be-cause.* |
| 269 | *forcolde.* MS: *for colde.* M, FP, F, B: *for-colde.* |
| 271 | *Qwyntyn.* M: *Gis certeyn.* FP: *Qisyntyn.* |
| 272 | *was.* M: *wos.* |
| 274 | *sethen.* M: emends to *seche* from *sechen.* |
| | *the.* MS, E, WA: *þe.* FP: *ȝe.* |
| after 274 | MS: in the bottom margin what appears to read *yris ynfull* is erased and the word *John* is written in the lower right corner in a different hand. |
| 275 | *And.* So E, L, C, WA. MS: *A.* M, FP, F: *I.* B: *A[nd].* |
| | *evyn wery.* So C. MS: *wery wery.* M, FP: *ewyn wery wery.* F, L: *even very weary.* B: *evyn very wery.* WA: *ewyn wery.* |
| 276 | *ageyn.* MS: *a geyn.* |
| | *to-morn.* So E, B, C, WA. MS: *to morrow.* L: *tomorn.* M: emends to *to-morne* from *to morow.* FP: *to-morow.* F: *to-morrow.* |
| 278 | *anon.* MS: *a non.* FP: *a-non.* |
| | *make.* M, FP: *made.* |
| | *avaunte.* M emends to this from *avaunce.* MS: *a vaunute.* |
| 280 | *unkynde.* MS: *o wnkynde.* |
| 281–85 | MS: *John* is written three times in the right margin next to these lines in a different hand. |
| 282 | *bowte.* FP: *sowte.* B: *bow[gh]te.* |
| 286 | *in.* So M, F, E, B, L, C. MS, FP: *&.* WA: *[in].* |
| 288 | *triede.* M: *lede.* |
| 289 | *fragylyté.* M: *fraylyte.* B: *fragilité.* |
| 290 | MS: *ita factum est* is written in a different hand in the right margin next to this line. M, FP, F: *sit.* B₂ suggests this is meant to replace the *ita* above *placuit* in line 292. |
| 292 | WA counts this line as two lines. |
| | *placuit.* MS: the letters *ita* are included above *placuit* but cancelled. |
| 294 | *Beware.* MS, WA, C: *Be ware.* M, FP: *Be-ware.* |
| 296 | *yowr.* MS, FP: *þer.* M: emends to *yower* from *Ther.* |
| | *all the.* So C. MS, FP: *all þer.* F, L: *all their.* E, WA: *all þe.* M, B: *all ther.* |
| | *menys.* FP: emends to this from *nnenys.* |

| | |
|---|---|
| 297 | *intromytt not yowrsylff.* MS: scribe alters this from *intyrmyse yowr sylff not.* F: *intermise yourself not.* |
| 298 | *this.* So C. MS: *þi.* FP, WA: *þi[s].* E: *þis.* F, B, M: *thi[s].* |
| 300 | *kepe.* M: emends to *this* from *kefe.* |
| 301 | *Beware.* MS, WA, C: *Be ware.* M, FP: *Be-ware.* |
| | *for.* So M, F, E, L, C. MS: *fo.* FP, B, WA: *fo[r].* |
| | *no.* MS: emends to *this* from *us.* |
| 303 | *befor.* MS: *be for.* M, FP: *be-for.* |
| | *ey.* So M, E, B, C, WA. MS, FP: *eyn.* F: *eyne.* |
| 305 | *Yf.* M: *Yff.* |
| 307 | *schelde.* So C, E. MS: *schede.* M, FP, B, WA: *sche[l]de.* F: *shie[l]d.* |
| | *fon.* M: emends to *this* from *son.* |
| 309 | *thes.* M: *yower,* suggests *yow.* B: *thes[e].* |
| | *worschyppull.* M: *worschypfull.* FP, C: *worschypp[ʃ]ull.* B: *worschipp[ʃ]ull.* |
| 312 | *worschyppfull.* M: *worschypfull.* B: *worschippfull.* |
| after 312 | MS: a now illegible line has been smudged out in the bottom margin. |
| 314 | *Thankynge.* M: emends to *Thankyd.* |
| | *be.* FP: *be [to].* C: *be to.* |
| | *commynge.* M, FP, C: *connynge.* F, L: *cunning.* B: *comminge.* |
| | *kam.* So MS, WA, B. F, L: *can.* C: *kan.* M, FP: emend to *kan* from *kam.* |
| 316 | *promycyon.* F: *promotion.* |
| 319 | *remors.* MS, E, WA: *remos.* M, FP, B, C: *remo[r]s.* F: *remo[r]se.* |
| 320 | *superstycyus.* M: *superstycyous.* B: *superstici[o]us.* |
| 321 | *in cinerem.* M: *[in] cinere[m].* |
| 323 | *goode.* MS: ~~god~~ *goode.* FP: *Gode.* |
| | MS: in the left margin next to this line the word *John* appears in a different hand. |
| 325 | *quam.* M: emends to *this* from *quiam.* |
| | *jocundum.* M: emends to *iocundum* from *Iocundie.* |
| 326 | *unum.* M: *uno.* |
| | MS: in the left margin next to this line the word *John* appears in a different hand. |
| 327 | *I her.* M: *Ther.* |
| | *hym.* MS: ~~hym~~ *hym.* |
| 328 | *erth.* MS: ~~erth~~ *erth.* |
| 329 | *ydullnes.* M: emends to *ydullnes* from *yeullnes.* |
| 330 | *yt hys.* M: emends to *hys* from *þat hys.* |
| 336–442 | M omits these lines. |
| 336 | *NOWADAYS.* MS: *nowad;* also true in lines 338, 340, and 342. |
| | *wyth a colle.* MS: scribe indicates the repetition in this line with a flourish. |
| 338 | *NEW GYSE.* MS: *newgys;* also true in line 790. |
| | *He that schytyth wyth hys hoyll.* MS: scribe indicates the repetition in this line with a flourish. |
| 339 | *wype hys ars clen.* MS: scribe indicates the repetition in this line with a flourish. |
| 341 | *yt shall be sen.* MS: scribe indicates the repetition in this line with a flourish. |
| 342 | *breche.* MS: ~~hys~~ *breche.* |
| | *breche yt shall be sen.* MS: *cetera* (second occurence). |

| | |
|---|---|
| 344 | *spade.* M: emends to this from *space.* |
| 346 | *this.* So B, L, C, M. MS: *þs.* E, FP, WA: *þis.* F: *is.* |
| | MS: in the left margin next to this line a *J* appears in a different hand. |
| after 350 | MS: in the bottom left corner of the folio *John* is written in a different hand. What appears to have been another *John* is smudged out in the center of the bottom margin. |
| 351 | *lat.* M: emends to *late* from *eat.* B, C: *lat[e].* |
| 356 | *Alasse.* MS: *A lasse.* FP: *A-lasse.* |
| 358 | *alonne.* MS: *a lonne.* M, FP: *a-lonne.* |
| 371 | *Yyt.* C, L: *Yet.* MS, E, M, FP, WA: *ʒyt.* |
| | *polytyke.* MS: *k polytyke.* |
| 373 | *Yf.* MS: *ħ yf.* |
| 374 | *Ande.* M: emends to this from *Arde.* |
| | *compasse.* M: emends to *compost.* FP, B: *compass[t]e.* WA: *comppasse.* F: *compos[t].* |
| 379 | *wolde.* M: *wolle.* |
| 381 | *NEW GYSE.* MS: *New g or.* Also true in lines 429, 441, 466, 479, 719, 775, and 808. |
| | *jewellys.* MS: *Iewellys.* M: *iewelles.* FP: *Jewelles.* |
| 385 | *shuld.* MS, FP: *xull.* F: *shall.* M: emends to *xulde* from *xall.* |
| 386 | *to.* According to E, the *t* is changed from another letter. |
| Before 388 | MS: illegible writing in a different hand has been smudged out in the top and left margins. |
| 392 | *thanke.* MS: *tæ thanke.* |
| 393 | *Blyssyde.* M: *B[l]yssyde.* |
| 394 | *the subsyde.* MS, E, WA: *þe subsyde.* M: emends to *this spade* from *By the fesyde.* FP: *þe syde,* suggests *ayde.* F: *aid.* B: *the subsidé.* |
| 395 | *Thre.* M: emends to this from *iij.* MS, FP: *iij.* |
| 397 | *hasta.* So M, FP, F, E, B, L, C. MS: *hastu.* WA: *hast[a].* |
| | *Dominus.* M: emends to this from *ons* with a line above it, i.e., *mons.* |
| 402 | *nere.* M: *rere.* |
| 404 | *Ande.* MS: *and Ande.* M: *And.* |
| | *agayn.* MS: *a gayn.* FP: *a-gayn.* |
| 405 | *convycte.* M: emends to this from *convytte.* |
| | *them.* MS, E, FP, WA: *þem.* MS: *þ* written below the line, *em* above two vertical lines, which are cancelled. |
| 407 | *resyst.* M: *re[s]yst.* |
| 409 | *worschyppull.* M: emends to *worschypfull.* FP, C: *worschypp[f]ull.* B: *worschipp[f]ull.* |
| 411 | *fett.* M emends to this from *sett.* L: *fetch.* |
| 414 | *Alasse.* MS: *A lasse.* M: *A-lasse.* M: *Alasse.* |
| | *I am wers.* So C. MS, E: *I wers.* M, FP, B, WA: *I [am] wers.* F: *I [am] worse.* L: *I am wrose.* |
| | *then.* MS, E, FP: *þen.* M: *the[n].* |
| 416 | *ondon.* MS: *on don.* M, FP: *on-don.* |
| 420 | *ageyn.* MS: *a geyn.* M, FP: *a-geyn.* |
| 422 | *New Gyse, Nowadays.* MS: *neugyse, nowad.* M: *New Gyse, Now-a-days.* B: *New-G[u]ise, Nowad[ays, and].* |
| | *hath.* FP, F, B: *hath [he].* L, C: *he hath.* |

|  | *to-beton.* So E, WA, C. MS: *to beton.* M, B: *to-betyn.* FP: *to-beten.* |
|---|---|
| before 426 | MS: *Honorabyll & well be lovyd frende I hertely Recummend me on to yow* is written in the top margin in a different hand. |
| 426 | *Alac, Alac!* MS: *A lac A lac.* M, FP: *A-lac! a-lac!* B: *Alac[k], alac[k]!* |
| 429 | *NEW GYSE.* MS: *Newg.* |
|  | *Alasse.* MS: *A lasse.* M: *A-lasse.* |
| 430 | *Alake!* MS: *a lake.* M: *A-lake.* B: *Ala[c]ke.* |
| 441 | *NEW GYSE.* MS: *Newg.* |
| 442 | *Cristys.* MS: *crastys.* M: emends to *Cristes* from *Craftes.* FP: *Cristis.* |
|  | *crose.* M: suggests *cross* or *curse.* |
|  | *awey.* MS: *a wey.* M, FP: *a-wey.* |
| 443 | *Ther wer on and on.* So E. MS, FP: *Ther wher on & on.* M: *Ther wer on anon.* F: *There! we're on anon.* B: *Ther, wher, on and on?* L: *There! Where? On and on!* C: *Ther wer on[e] and on[e]!* WA: *Ther? Where on? and on?* |
| 446 | *recumbentibus.* M: emends to this from *recumtenibus.* |
| 451 | *out.* M, B, C: *ou[gh]t.* F, L: *aught.* |
| 452 | *in.* F: *on.* |
| 453 | *apase.* MS: *a pase.* M, FP: *a-pase.* |
|  | *flewte.* M: queries *flowte.* F, B: *flowte.* |
| 456 | *si dedero.* M: emends to this from *Tidedere.* F: *si didero.* |
| 457 | *Ye.* MS, WA, FP: *ȝo.* F: *So!* L: *Yea.* M, E: *ȝe.* |
|  | *wey.* MS: *þᵢ wey.* |
|  | *onto.* MS: *on to.* M, FP: *on-to.* F, L: *unto.* |
| 458 | *ther.* MS, E, FP, WA: *þer.* M: emends to *ther* from *thei.* |
| 461 | *that ys of.* So C. MS: *þat of.* E: *þat ys.* F, B: *that [is] of.* WA, FP: *þat [is] of.* M: *that of.* |
| 462 | *NOWADAYS.* MS: *Nowad.* B: *NOWAD[AYS].* |
|  | *Kepe.* MS: *þ kepe.* |
| 463 | *worschyppull.* M: emends to *worschypfull.* FP, C: *worschypp[f]ull.* B: *worschipp[f]ull.* |
| 464 | *or.* So FP. M: emends to this from *of.* MS, E, B, L, C, WA : *of.* F: *nor.* |
|  | *to.* B, C: *t[w]o.* M, FP: *to-pens.* L: *tuppence.* |
| 470 | *alyke.* MS: *a lyke.* M, FP: *a-lyke.* |
| 471 | *NOUGHT.* So M. MS: *Nough.* FP, B: *NOUGH[T].* |
| 474 | *beware.* MS, E, FP, C: *be ware.* M: *be-ware.* |
| 475 | *dominancium.* F, B, L: *dominantium.* M: emends to *dominantium* from *duancum.* |
| 477 | *hem.* So E. MS, M, FP: *hym.* F: *him.* |
| 480 | *to.* MS, M, FP: *ii.* C: *t[w]o.* B: *two.* |
| 481 | *was.* M: *wos.* |
| 482 | *thi.* MS: *þᵢs þi.* E, FP, WA: *þi.* |
| 483 | *have thee qwytt.* MS: *have quyll.* M, FP: *haue [the] qwyll.* F: *have [thee]! While.* E: *haue the qwytt.* B: *[the] qwitt.* WA: *have the[e] qwy[tt].* L: *have the whit!* C: *have the qwytt!* |
| 487 | *Non.* So L, E, C, WA. MS: *No.* M, FP, B, F: *No[n].* |
| 490 | MS: scribe repeated the line to the right and then cancelled it. |
| 491 | *ys.* MS: a *t* appears in a lighter ink before *ys.* |
| 493 | *yt.* FP: *þat [yt].* F: *that.* M: *that [yt].* B: *[that] it.* |

| | |
|---|---|
| 497 | *fyve vowellys.* So E, C, WA. MS, FP: *.v. vowellys.* B: *five vowellys.* M: *v voli ellys,* queries *vij* or *xx devellys.* F: *five vowels.* |
| 498 | *the sytyca.* MS, E, FP, WA: *þe sytyca.* M: *tye sytica,* queries *the syatica.* L: *the sciatica.* B: *the si[a]tica.* |
| 500 | *hat.* M, B, F: *hat[h].* |
| | *informyde.* FP, B: *informyde [me].* F: *informed [me].* L: *informed me.* |
| 501 | *make.* FP: *made.* |
| | *a vow.* FP, M: *a-vow.* E, WA: *avow.* |
| 503 | *William Fyde.* So E, C. MS: *w ffyde.* M: emends to *w[ith yow] Fyde* from *Iake w . . . Fyde.* FP, WA, B: *W[illiam] Fyde.* F, L: *W[illiam] Fide.* |
| 505 | *Sauston.* FP, F: *Sanston.* M: emends to *Sanston* from *sansten.* |
| 506 | *Wylliam.* M: *Wyllam.* B: *William.* |
| | *Hauston.* So MS, E, B. M, FP, F: *Hanston.* L: *Hauxton.* |
| 509 | *Waltom.* M, F, B, L: *Walton.* |
| 511 | *Fullburn.* MS: *h fullburn.* F, L: *Fulbourn.* |
| before 512 | MS: *yy* is written in the left margin before this line. |
| 512 | *ys a.* MS: written above *va.* |
| 516–17 | These lines are reversed in the manuscript but are restored in this edition, following F, E, B, L, C, and WA for sense and rhyme. M and FP do not alter the manuscript order. |
| 518 | *be.* M: emends to *se.* F: *see.* |
| | *ware wethere.* So E, B, WA, C. MS: *ware & wethere.* M, FP: *ware & wether.* F: *where and whither.* L: *ware whither.* |
| 520 | *con.* So E, F, B, L, C, WA. MS: *com.* M, FP: emend to *con* from *com.* |
| | *that.* MS: *þat* is squeezed between *verse* and *we.* |
| | *cheke.* M: emends to this from *choke.* |
| 522 | *lyfte.* MS: ~~ryght~~ *lyfte.* |
| | *befall.* MS: *be fall.* M, FP: *be-fall.* |
| 523 | *agayn.* MS: *a gayn.* M, FP: *a-geyn.* |
| 524 | *And.* So E, L, C. MS: *A.* M: *A[nde].* FP, WA, F, B: *A[nd].* |
| | *avantage.* MS: *a vantage.* M, FP: *a-vantage.* |
| 525 | *tary.* MS: ~~be~~ *tary.* |
| 526 | *asyde.* MS: *a syde.* M, FP: *a-syde.* |
| 527 | *be hys gyde.* M: *[be] hys syde.* WA: *by hys gyde.* B: *be his g[u]ide.* |
| 529 | *invysybull.* MS: *in vysybull.* |
| | *jett.* M: *rett.* |
| 530 | *Ande.* So E, M, FP, WA, C, B. MS: *A.* F, L: *And.* |
| | *befor.* MS: *be for.* M, FP: *be-for.* |
| 531 | *fote-mett.* M: *fote wett.* FP: *fote mett.* |
| 533 | *be.* M: emends to this from *he.* |
| | *hyde.* B: *hid[d]e.* |
| 534 | *onredyly.* MS: *on redyly.* FP: *ouer redyly,* suggests *on redyly.* M: emends to *on-redyly* from *ouer redyly.* |
| 535 | *assayde.* M: *a-wayde,* queries *assayde.* |
| 537 | *drawke.* M: *draw.* FP, F, L: *drawk.* |
| 538 | *sow.* M: emends to this from *sew.* |
| 540 | *wane.* MS: ~~wane~~ *cum.* Accoring to E, this is in a later hand. |

543    *Qwyll I overdylew yt.* MS: *Qwyll I ouer dylew yt.* M: *I wyll ron dylewer, that.* B:
       *Qw[h]ill I over-dylve it.*
544    *Filii.* M: emends to this from *filius.*
       *begyn.* M, FP: *be-gyn.*
545    *unlusty.* MS: *wn lusty.* FP: *wn-lusty.*
546    *at wynter.* F, FP: *at wyntur.* B: *at vyntur.* L: *at a venture.* C: *at aventur.*
547    *Alasse.* MS: *A lasse.* M, FP: *A-lasse.*
555    MS: below the speech marker of *Titivillus, nev g* is written apparently
       assigning the speech to New Guise. This also occurs in Titivillus' next two
       speeches starting at lines 565 and 589.
556    *ageyn.* MS: *a geyn.* M, FP: *a-geyn.*
557    *Qwyst.* So FP. M: *I-wyst.* F: *Whist.* B: *Qw[h]ist!*
561    *into.* MS: *in to.* M: *in-to.*
       *thi.* MS, E, WA: *þi.* FP: *þi[s].* L, C: *the.* M, F, B: *thi[s].*
       *ageyn.* MS: *a geyn.* M, FP: *a-geyn.*
562    MS: the scribe first wrote and then cancelled line 564: *My bedys xall be here*
       *for who sum euer wyll ellys.*
564    *bedys.* M: emends to *bedes* from *ledes.* FP: *bedis.*
       *ellys.* So E, B, WA, C. MS, M, FP: *cumme,* but *ellys,* which rhymes with
       *compellys* in line 560, was written before line 562.
565    *TITIVILLUS.* MS: *TITYUI.*
       *dyde.* M: emends to this from *eyde.*
566    *He.* MS: *B he.*
567    *Iwysse.* MS, WA: *I wysse.* M, FP: *I-wysse.*
570    *powder.* So E, C, WA. MS: *power.* M, FP, F, B: *pow[d]er.*
573    *ageyn.* MS: *a geyn.* M, FP: *a-geyn.*
575    *asyde.* MS: *a syde.* M, FP: *a-syde.*
576    *a.* M, FP: *[se] a.* F: *[see] a.*
       *sport.* M: emends to this from *spert.*
577    *ageyn.* MS: *a geyn.* M, FP: *a-geyn.*
578    *I.* MS: *A I.*
579    *abroche.* MS: *a broche.* M, FP: *a-broche.*
580    *asyde.* MS: *a syde.* M, FP: *a-syde.*
581    *MANKYNDE.* MS: *MAN;* also true in lines 585, 607, 706, 717, and 819.
       *Evynsong.* MS, E: *Ewynsong.* M, FP: *Ewynsonge.*
583    *over.* FP, F: *on.*
584–86 MS: these lines are added at the foot of the page with marks to indicate
       their proper placement in the text.
584    *as be.* F: *as it.*
       *another.* MS: *a noþer.* M: *a-nother.* FP: *a-noþer.* WA: *anoþer.*
586    *thow.* B: *thow[gh].* M: emends to *thowgh* from *then.*
588    *slepe.* M: emends to this from *skope.* FP: queries *skepe.*
       *wore.* M, FP, F, B, L: *were.*
589    *for me.* F: *me.*
590    *worde.* M: *werde.*
591    *praty.* M: emends to this from *pauty.*
       *scheude.* M: emends to *schowde* from *schende.* B: *schewde.*

| | |
|---|---|
| 592 | *aslepe.* MS: *a slepe.* M: emends to *on slepe* from *& sleep.* FP: *a-slepe.* |
| 593 | *Qwyst!* M: *I-wyst.* F, L: *Whist.* B: *Qw[h]ist.* |
| | *ys.* MS: ~~yd~~ *ys.* |
| 594 | *Alasse.* MS: *A lasse.* FP: *A-lasse.* |
| | *alasse.* MS: *a lasse.* FP: *a-lasse!* |
| 595 | *away.* MS: *a way.* M, FP: *a-way.* |
| 597 | *as.* So M, E, FP, F, B, L, C, WA. MS: *ab.* |
| 598 | *on.* M, FP: *ouer.* F: *over.* |
| | *galous.* MS: written as *galouf,* with the *f* cancelled and an *s* added above the rest of the word. E, C, WA: *galouse.* M, FP: emend to *galous* from *galouf.* B: *galows.* |
| 599 | *Bycause.* MS: *By cause.* M, FP: *By-cause.* |
| 601 | *beforn.* MS: *be forn.* M, FP: *be-forn.* |
| 602 | *Aryse.* MS: *A ryse.* M, FP: *A-ryse.* |
| 603 | *cun.* M, FP: *cum.* F: *come.* |
| | *avyse.* MS: *a vyse.* M, FP: *A-vyse.* |
| 604 | MS: *leve* is written in the left margin before the rest of the line. |
| | *brethell.* M: *brechell,* queries *brethell.* FP: *[be] brethell,* queries *be left.* |
| 605 | *Farwell.* So E, C. MS: *ffor well.* FP: *For well.* F, L: *Farewell.* M, B: *For-well.* WA: *Forwell.* |
| 607 | *avows.* MS, M: *a vows.* FP: *a-vows.* |
| 609 | *Adew.* MS: *A dew.* M, FP: *A-dew.* |
| | *masters.* M, FP: *mastere,* FP queries *mastere[s].* F: *master.* |
| 611 | *And.* So E, L, C. MS: *A.* M: *A[nde].* FP, WA, F, B: *A[nd].* |
| 613 | *overron.* MS: *ouer ron.* FP, M, F: *on! run!* B: *over-ron.* |
| 616 | *asonder.* MS: *a sonder.* M: *a-sondre.* FP: *asondur.* |
| 617 | *abowte.* MS: *a bowte.* M, FP: *a-bowte.* |
| 618 | *Beware.* MS: *Be ware.* M, FP: *Be-ware.* |
| 621 | *Alasse.* MS: *A lasse.* M, FP: *A-lasse.* |
| | *lyghly.* FP: *lygh[t]ly.* F: *likely.* M: *lyghtly.* |
| 624 | *Alasse.* MS: *A lasse.* M, FP: *A-lasse.* |
| | *neke.* M: emends to this from *nekes.* |
| | *make.* M: emends to this from *made.* |
| | *avowe.* MS: *a vowe.* M: *a-vowe.* |
| 625 | *MANKYNDE.* MS: *M*; also true in lines 627, 709, 713, and 899. B: *M[ANKIND].* |
| 627 | *that.* MS, E, WA: *þat.* FP: *þer.* F: *there.* M: *ther.* |
| | *abowte.* MS: *a bowte.* |
| 628 | *Audyrs.* M: *Andrys.* FP, WA, C: *Audrys.* L: *Audrey's.* |
| 629 | *dyshes.* F: *dishele.* L: *disease.* |
| 630 | *ryngeworme.* MS: *rynge worme.* M, FP: *rynge-worme.* |
| 631 | *arom.* MS, FP: *a rom.* B: *a-rom.* |
| 634–37 | MS: as the stanzas in this section of the play are all eight lines rhyming *aaabcccb,* and this one lacks a *c* rhyme, there may be a line missing here. |
| 636 | *Avante.* MS: *A vante.* M, FP: *A-vante.* |
| 637 | *geet.* M: *gret.* |
| 641 | *scoryde.* So FP. M: *sco[w]ryde.* F: *sco[u]red.* L: *scoured.* B: *sco[u]ryde.* |

642 MS: below the speech marker of *Myscheff*, *novad* is written, apparently assigning the speech to Nowadays. This also occurs in line 664.

645 *the*. MS, E, WA: *þe*. F: *that*. FP: *þo*. M: emends to *that* from *the*.

646 *owyn*. So M. MS, E, WA: *owȝn*. FP: *owȝun*.

647 *awey*. MS: *a wey*. M, FP: *a-wey*.

648 *anow*. MS: *a now*. M: *a-non*. FP: *a-now*. L: *enow*. F: *enou'*.

649 *chesance*. F: *che[vi]sance*. B: *chesa[u]nce*.

652 *yow*. MS: *w* is blotted.
*amendys*. MS: *a mendys*. M: *a-mendes*. FP: *a-mendis*.

656 *thre*. MS, M, FP: *iij*.

658 *amysse*. MS: *a mysse*. M, FP: *a-mysse*.

663 *Mankyndys*. M: *Mankynde*. FP: *Mankyndis*. WA: *Mankynds*.

664 *a*. MS: *ȝt a*.

665 MS: this line is written to the right of 664 and 665. M, FP, F, and L print this line as a stage direction.
*mak*. MS: *þ mak*.

666 *And*. So E, L, C, WA. MS, FP: *A*. F: *Ah*. M: *A[nde]*. B: *A[nd]*.
*sub*. M: emends to *in* from *se*. FP: *fo*.
*dasarde*. M: *desarde*. F: *d'hasard*. B: *das[t]arde*.

667 MS, M, FP print this as two lines.
*Oyyt*. So C. MS: *O y yt*. M: *Oy yt*. FP: *Oy-yt!* F, L: *Oyez*.
*Oyyt*. MS: *Oy ȝyt*. M, WA: *Oy yȝt*. C: *Oyyy*. E: *Oyȝyt*. FP: *Oy-yȝt*. F, L: *Oyez*.
*Oyet*. So C. MS: *ȝyt*. FP: *O yet*. F, L: *Oyez*. WA: *Oyȝyt*.
*women*. MS: *womæn*.

670 MS: below the speech marker of *Mischief*, *novad* is written, apparently assigning the speech to Nowadays.

672 *jakett*. M: emends to *iackett* from *rakett*.
*tolde*. So FP, B, M, E. F: *sold*.

675 *Ande*. So MS, E, C, WA, M, FP, B. F, L: *And*.
*ageyn*. MS: *a geyn*. M, FP: *a-geyn*.
*in ony*. M: emends to this from *for in ony*.

678 *And*. So E, L, C. MS: *A*. M: *A[nde]*. FP, WA, F, B: *A[nd]*.
*mow*. So E, B, L, C, WA. M: emends to this from *may*. MS, FP, F: *may*.

680 MS: below the speech marker of *Mischief*, *novad* is written, apparently assigning the speech to Nowadays.

682 MS: this line is written in the right margin.
*I beschrew*. MS: *I be schrew*. M: *Be-schrew*. FP: *I be-shrew*.
*a*. So MS, M. FP: *&*.

683 *rennynge*. So M, F, E, L, C, WA. MS: *rennyge*. B: *renn[i]nge*. FP: *renny[n]ge*.
*fyst*. M: emends to this from *syft*.

686 *hede*. MS: *h hede*.
*stoude*. M, FP: *stonde*. F: *stand*. L: *stands*.

687 *Carici*. So MS, E, C, WA. M: *Garici*. FP, F, B, L: *Curia*.
*tenta*. M: *tota*.

690 *nullateni*. MS: this word is written in the right margin but marked for proper placement in the text. So E, B. M, F: *millatene*, M queries *nullatene*. FP: *millateni*. L: *nulliateni*.

| | |
|---|---|
| 692 | *As*. M: *Do*, queries *Lo* or *So*. |
| 693–94 | MS: as there is no rhyme for *nullateni* in line 690, a line appears to be missing here. |
| 694 | *taryynge*. So E, L, C. M: *[taryyng]*. FP: *tarrynge*. B: *[taryinge]*. WA: *[taryynge]*. F: *[tarrying]*. MS: this line should end with a rhyme for *ferthynge* in line 695 and *fyghtynge* in line 696; MS ends with *moche*. |
| 703 | *goo to*. M: *goo [to]*. |
| | *aboute*. MS: *a boute*. M, FP: *a-boute*. |
| 704 | *Onto*. MS: *On to*. M, FP: *On-to*. F, L: *Unto*. |
| | *goodewyff*. MS, FP: *goode wyff*. M: *goode-wyff*. B: *goode-wife*. |
| | *goodeman*. MS, FP: *goode man*. M, B: *goode-man*. |
| 705 | *MANKYNDE*. M: emends to *Mank* from *M*. |
| 712 | *And*. So M, E, L, C, WA. MS: *A*. FP, B, F: *A[nd]*. |
| | *forbere*. MS: *for bere*. M: emends to *forber* from *A for bef*. FP: *for-ber*. |
| 715 | *onbrace*. MS: *on brace*. M, FP: *on-brace*. |
| 716 | *thus*. M: *tans*. |
| | *overface*. MS, M: *ouer face*. FP: *ouer-face*. |
| 719 | *jake of fence*. MS: *Iake*. M: *iake[tt] of s[er]u[i]ce*. B: *jake[t] of fence*. L: *jake-of-fence*. |
| 720 | *Hay*. F: *Hi*. |
| | *doog*. M: *doo ye*. |
| 722 | *aspyede*. MS: *a spyede*. M, FP: *a-spyede*. WA, C, B: *aspyede*. |
| 724 | *beschrew*. MS: *be schrew*. M, FP: *be-schrew*. |
| 726 | *Fle*. M: emends to this from *sle*. C: *Fle[e]*. |
| 727 | *wyth thee*. MS: *wyth*. F, B: *with [thee]*. C: *wyth the[e]*. FP: *with [þee]*. WA: *wyth [þee]*. E: *wyth þe*. M: *with [the]*. |
| | *another*. MS: *a noþer*. M: *a-nother*. FP: *a-noþer*. WA: *anoþer*. |
| | *tyme*. So M, FP, E, C, WA. MS: *tym*. B: *tim[e]*. F, L: *time*. |
| 728 | *together*. MS: *to gether*. M, FP: *to-gether*. |
| 731 | *awey*. MS: *a wey*. M, FP: *a-wey*. |
| | *beschyte*. MS: *be schyte*. M, FP: *be-schyte*. B: *beschit[t]e*. |
| 732 | *football*. MS: *foot ball*. M, FP, F: *foot-ball*. |
| 733 | *anow*. MS: *a now*; true of all four instances in this line. C: *A, now!* M, FP, B: *a-now*. |
| 734 | *trymmelyth*. MS: ~~tri~~ *trymmelyth*. F: *tir-trimmeleth*. FP: *tir-trymmelyth*. L: *trembleth*. |
| 736 | *solace*. So M, FP, F, E, B. MS: *solalace*. |
| 737 | *Wythout*. MS: *Wyth out*. M, FP: *With-out*. |
| | *kan not*. So E, C. MS: *kan*. M, FP, WA: *kan [not]*. B: *kan[not]*. F, L: *can[not]*. |
| 740 | *afflixcyon*. M: *aff[l]ixyon*. |
| 742 | *onkynde*. MS: *on kynde*. M, FP: *on-kynde*. B: *on-kinde*. |
| 745 | *was*. So MS. M: *wos*. |
| 746 | *thin*. MS, FP: *þis*. M, F, L: *this*. E: *þin*. B: *thin[e]*. WA: *þ[in]*. |
| | *mutabylyté*. MS, FP: *imutabylyte*. B: *mutabilité*. |
| 748 | *oncurtess*. So E, C, WA. MS: *over curtess*. M: *on-curtess*. FP, B: *on-curtess*. |
| 750 | *thi*. MS, FP: *þis*. E, WA: *þi*. F, B: *thy*. M: *this*, queries *thi*. |
| 751 | *Thy*. So E, F, B, L, C, WA. MS, FP: *Thys*. M: *Thys*, queries *thy*. |
| | *cannot*. MS, M, E, WA, C: *can not*. |

752   *God and to.* So E, B, L, C. MS: *go on to.* WA: *Go[d] and to.* M: *go ouer.* FP: *go ouer to.* F: *go over, to.*

754   *et.* So M, FP, F, E, B, L, C, WA. MS: *sit.*
        *omnia.* M: emends to this from *sit oiat.*

755   MS: *Olyuer* is written in the right margin before this line.
        *ingratum.* MS: *in gratum.* M, FP: *in-gratum.*
        *lugent.* M, FP, F: *lugetur.*

758   *amytt.* M, FP: *a[d]mytt.* B: *A[d]mitt.* F: *admit.*

759   *Equyté.* M: emends to this from *O quyte.* B: *Equité.*
        *onparty.* MS: *on party.* M: emends to *pety* from *perty.* FP: *ouer party.* F: *over part[l]y.*

762   *ways.* MS: *ve ways.*

764   *caytyfs.* So FP, E, C. M: emends to this from *cayftys.* MS: *cayftys.* WA: *cay[tyf]s.* F, L: *caitiffs.* B: *caityfs.*

770   *proteccyon.* M, C: *protecyon.*

772   *fadere.* So MS, B. M, FP, F, L: *father.* E, C, WA: *fader.*
        *out.* MS, M, FP, E, C, WA: *owt.*
        *yowr.* FP: *yowur.* M: *yower.*

773   *to-gloryede.* MS: *to gloryede.* M: emends to *to-glosyede* from *gloryede.*

774   *ever.* MS, FP: *euer.* M: *ouer.* F: *over.*

775   According to M, a line may be missing here since there is no line to rhyme with *mynde* in line 778.

776   *Ny.* So FP, E, B, C, WA. M: emends to this from *my.* MS: *my.*

778   *overlong.* MS: *ouer long.* M: *ouer-longe.* FP: *ouer longe.* B: *over-long.*

779   *NOWADAYS.* MS: *Nowaday.*
        *dominus.* M, FP: *domine.*

780   *cape.* So M, E, B, L, C. MS, FP, F: *cepe.* WA: *c[a]pe.*
        *corpus.* So M, E, B, L, C, WA. M: emends to this from *coppus.* MS: *coppus?* FP, F: *coppus.*

782   *schett.* FP: *schott.* F: *shot.* M: *schotte.*

783   *beware.* MS, FP, WA, C: *be ware.* M: *be-ware.*

784   *arayde.* MS: *a rayde.* M, FP: *a-rayde.*

786   *overschett.* MS: *ouer schett.* M: *ouer-schott.* FP: *ouer-schett.* B: *over-schett.*

787   *behynde.* MS, M: *be hynde.* FP: *be-hynde.*

788   *belyve.* MS: *be lyue.* M, FP: *be-lyue.*
        *aferde.* MS: *a ferde.* M, FP: *a-ferde.*

792   *everywere.* MS: *euery were.* M: *euery-were.* FP: *euerywere.* B: *everyw[h]ere.*

793   *hymselff.* MS, FP: *hym selff.* M: *hym-selff.*

795   *Qwyppe.* M: *I Wyppe.* F: *I whip.* FP: *I-wyppe.* L: *Whip.*
        *anon.* MS: *a non.* M, FP: *a-non.*

796   *clothes.* MS, E, FP, WA: *clopes.* M: emends to *clowtes* from *clothes.* L: *clouts.*

798   *Kowde.* M: *Cowde.*

801   *Anon.* MS: *A non.* M, FP: *A-non.*

804   *thi.* MS, E, FP, WA: *þi.* M: emends to *the* from *þi.*

805   *thy.* So F, L, C. M: emends to this from *þye.* MS: *þye.* FP, E: *þy.* WA: *[þy].* B: *thye.*
        *avyse.* MS: *a vyse.* M: *a-vyse.*

| | |
|---|---|
| 806 | *thisylff.* MS, FP: *þi sylff.* E, WA: *þisylff.* M: *thi-sylff.* |
| 807 | *bales.* M: emends to *balef* from *bales.* L: *baleys.* |
| 808 | *Alass.* MS: *A lass.* M, FP: *A-lass.* |
| 810 | *Alasse.* MS: *A lasse.* M, FP: *A-lasse.* |
| 811 | *Aryse.* MS: *A ryse.* M, FP: *A-ryse.* |
| 812 | *ys.* So M, FP, E. MS: *ys ys.* |
| | *exspyre.* MS: *exspye.* FP: *expy[re].* F: *expi[re].* M: *expy[re].* |
| 813 | *Alasse.* MS: *A lasse.* |
| | *apere.* MS: *a pere.* M, FP: *a-pere.* |
| 814 | *solaycyose.* MS: an *a* added above the first *y.* M: emends to *solacyose* from *solycyose.* F: *solicitous.* |
| 816 | *yowrsylff.* So WA, C, B. MS: *yowr sylff.* M: *yower-sylff.* FP: *yowur sylff.* |
| 819 | MS: The last four pages are written in another hand. |
| | *agayn.* MS: *a gayn.* M: *a-geyn.* FP: *a-gayn.* |
| | *vyle.* So C. FP, M: *wyld,* M suggests *vile* or *vild.* F: *wild.* B, L: *vile.* |
| | *petycyun.* M: emends to *petysyon* from *pety syn.* FP: *petycyn.* |
| 820 | *yt ys.* FP: *þat ys.* M: *that ys.* F: *that is.* C: *that ys.* |
| 821 | *iterat.* M: emends to *wekit* from *werut.* FP: *werst.* F: *worst.* |
| 822 | *not.* MS: ~~nto~~ *not.* |
| 824 | *terys.* M: emends to *feres* from *seres.* FP: *feris.* F: *fears.* |
| | *amownt.* MS: *a mownt.* M, FP, B: *a-mownte.* |
| 825 | *pirssid.* So E, B. MS: *pirssie.* M, FP: *blyssed.* F: *blessed.* |
| | *redouce.* M: emends to *reduce* from *redeme.* FP: *redeme.* F: *redeem.* |
| 826 | *mutacio.* M: *mutaes.* B, F, L: *mutatio.* |
| | *dextre.* M: *dexire.* F: *dexteræ.* B, L: *dexterae.* |
| | *vertit.* M: *veint.* |
| 827 | *Aryse.* MS: *A ryse.* M, FP: *A-ryse.* |
| 829 | *exclude thee.* So L. MS: *exclude.* M: *exclude [the].* F, B, FP: *exclude [thee].* C, WA: *exclude the[e].* E: *exclude the.* |
| | *perpetuité.* MS: second *p* is added above the second *e.* M: *per[p]etuite.* |
| 830 | *ope.* M: emends to this from *ofe.* |
| 832 | *revyvyd.* MS: *rewyvyd* with *v* crowded in between surrounding letters. M: *reuyu[y]d.* |
| | *ageyn.* MS: *a geyn.* M, FP: *a-geyn.* |
| 833 | *Hymselfe.* MS, FP: *hym selfe.* M: *hym-sylfe.* WA: *Hymsylfe.* |
| | *preche.* So B, C. MS, FP, E, WA: *precyse.* M: *pre-cyse,* queries *preche* or *precysely teche* since the line should rhyme wih *wrech* in line 831. F: *precise.* L: *preach.* |
| 834 | *Nolo.* M: emends to this from *mole.* |
| | *inquit.* M: emends to this from *inquis.* FP: *inquit &.* |
| | *redusyble.* MS: *wyll redusyble;* ~~reducylle~~ by a later hand and *reducyble* added. F, E, B, L, C, WA: add *be.* M, FP: *[be] reducyble.* |
| 835 | *ys.* MS: ~~hy~~ *ys.* |
| | *wythowte.* MS: *wyth owte.* M: *wyth-owt.* FP: *wyth-owte.* |
| 836 | *were mercy.* M, L: *where Mercy.* B: *w[h]ere mercy.* |
| 839 | *onto.* MS: *on to.* M: emends to *on-to* from *peruyon to.* FP: *on-to.* F, L: *unto.* |
| 841 | *Trowthe.* M: emends to this from *Growthe.* |

*argument.* M: emends to this from *acgmmes.*

842    *contraversye.* M: *controuersaye.* FP: *controuersye.*

843    *Aryse.* M: emends to *Ryse* from *Byse.*

844    *Inclyne yowyr capacité; my doctrine ys convenient.* FP, E, B, L, C: emend to this
         for rhyme. MS: *My doctrine ys conuenient Inclyne yowyr capacite.* M: *Inclyne
         yowur capacite, my doctrine ys conuenient.*

845    *notary.* M: *notarie.*

847    *ye thynke.* MS, WA: *ȝe thynke.* M: omits.

848    *The.* So FP, F, E, B, L, C, WA. MS: *They.* M: emends to *The* from *Then.*

851    *preservyd.* So B, C. M: *preseruyt.* FP: *preseruyd.*

        *avowtry.* MS: *a wowtry.* M, FP: *a-wowtry.* F: *advoutry.*

854    *I.* So M, FP, E, F, B, L, C. MS: *he.* WA: *[I].*

856    *anon.* MS: *a non.* M, FP: *a-non.*

858    *grevans.* MS: the *s* is writen over a *g.* M: emends to *grevance* from *grewange.*
         FP: *grewance.*

860    *expedycius.* M: emends to this from *expedicies.*

        *insyght.* MS: *in syght.* M: *in-syght.*

862    *quadrantem.* M emends to this from *quadrute[m].*

        *schall.* So C. MS: *scha.* M, FP, E, B, WA: *scha[ll].* F: *sha[ll].* L: *shall.*

        *your.* MS, E, WA: *ȝour.* FP: *þis.* M, F: *this.*

863    *sowle.* So E, C, WA. MS: *sowe.* M: *sow[l]s.* FP, B: *sow[l]e.*

        *hys.* So M, FP, C, E, WA. MS: *yys.*

864    *dyscesse.* M: *dysesse.*

865    *thynke.* MS: *ȝ thynke.*

866    *Ecce.* M: emends to this from *Este.*

        *acceptabile.* M: emends to this from *aucptabile.*

867    *word.* So MS, E, WA. M, FP, B, C, F: *wor[l]d.* L: *world.*

868    *above.* MS: *a bowe.* M: *a-boue.* FP: *a-bowe.*

869    *lest.* MS: *ħ lest.* M, FP: *holest,* M suggests *loliest* or *lest.* F: *lowli'st.*

        *kevyn.* MS: *hewyn.* M: *heuyn.*

870    *prove.* FP: *prewe.*

871    *suavius.* FP: *suatius.* M: emends to *solatius* from *suatius.*

873    *wythowte.* MS: *wyth owte.* M, FP: *wyth-owte.*

874    *inexcusabyll.* M: emends to this from *inexousobyll.* M, FP: query *inexorable.*

875    *swemyth.* M: *siremyth,* queries *sore nyeth.*

        *onwysely.* MS: *on wysely.* M, FP: *on-wysely.*

876    *Tytivillus.* F: *Titivilly.* M, FP: *Tytiuilly.*

        *my.* MS: *ȝ my.*

877    *sediciusly.* M, F: *sedulously.* FP: *sedociusly.* B: *sedici[o]usly.*

878    *To.* FP: *Be.* M: emends to *He* from *Be.* F: *By.*

        *Nowadayis.* M: *Now-a-days.* FP: *Now-a-dayis.*

        *Nowght.* M: *Nought.*

879    *oblivyows.* M: *obliuyous.* FP: *obliuyows.*

        *monytorye.* So E, C. MS: *manyterge.* M: *marytorye.* FP: *manyterye.* F: *manitory.*
         WA: *m[o]nytor[y]e.*

880    *before.* MS: *be fore.* M, FP: *be-fore.*

        *Titivillus.* F: *Titivilly.* M, FP: *Titiuilly.*

|            | *asay.* MS: *a say.* M, FP: *a-say.* |
|------------|--------------------------------------|
| 882        | *prestita.* So E. M: *perfectum.* FP, F: *prefata.* B, L: *praestita.* |
|            | *minus.* M: *non.* |
| 883        | *thre.* MS, M, FP: *iij.* |
|            | *and he.* M, FP, F: *he.* |
|            | *mayster.* M, FP: *master.* |
|            | *hem.* M: *[t]hem.* F: *them.* |
| 884        | *and the Fell.* So C, B. MS: *and þe ffell.* E, WA: *and þe Fell.* M: *& [I] the tell.* FP: *& þe Fell.* |
| 885        | *The.* M: *That.* |
|            | *Nowgth.* M: *& Nought.* |
|            | *hem.* M: *[t]hem.* F: *them.* |
| 886        | *propyrly.* So E, C. MS: *propylly.* M, FP, B: *propy[r]lly.* WA: *propy[r]ly.* F: *prope[r]ly.* |
|            | *Titivillus.* F: *Titivilly.* M, FP: *Titiuilly.* |
|            | *syngnyfyth.* M: *syngnyf[ie]th.* FP: *syngnyfyes.* B: *singnifith.* |
| 888        | *thre.* MS, M, FP: *iij.* |
| 889        | *temporall.* M: *temperull.* FP: *temperall.* |
| 890        | *before.* MS: this word is written above *a mong,* which is cancelled. M: omits. |
|            | *worscheppyll.* E: *worscheppyll.* M: *worschypfyll.* FP: *worschypp[ſ]yll.* F: *worschip[ſ]ul.* B: *worchepp[ſ]yll.* |
| 892        | *fro.* MS: ~~syro~~ *fro.* |
|            | *evermore.* MS: *euer more.* M, FP: *euer-more.* |
| 894        | *Libere.* WA: *Liebere.* |
|            | *welle.* M, F, C: *velle.* |
|            | *libere.* So M, F, E, B, L, C, FP, WA. MS: *liebere.* |
|            | *nolle.* M, F: *velle.* FP: *welle.* |
|            | *iwys.* MS: *i wys.* M, FP: *i-wys.* |
| 895        | *Titivillus.* FP: *Tityuilly.* F: *Titivilly.* M: *Titiuilly.* |
|            | *enmys.* MS: This word is written above what appears to be *his Impryse,* which is cancelled. M: queries *enuius.* FP: *enuyus.* B: *envi[o]us.* F, L: *envious.* |
| 898        | *persverans.* MS: *s perseverans.* WA, C: *perseverans.* |
| after 898  | MS: in the bottom margin various letters and what appears to read *skrypture* are written. |
| before 899 | MS: *Olyuer* is written in the upper right margin. |
| 899        | *MANKYNDE:* MS: *MAN,* with last two letters hidden by tape. B: *M[ANKIND].* |
| 901        | *Dominus.* M: emends to this from *Domine.* |
|            | *custodit.* M, FP, F: *custodi[a]t.* |
|            | *malo.* M: emends to this from *mali.* |
| 902        | *Filii.* M: emends to this from *filiis.* FP: *Filij.* |
| 903        | *Wyrschepyll.* M, FP, B: *Wyrschep[ſ]yll.* F refers to lines from this point on as the "Epilogue." |
| 904        | *deliveryd.* So WA. MS: *deliueryd,* the *u* may be written over another letter. |
|            | *faverall.* M: *sunerall,* queries *special.* FP: *suuerall.* F: *several.* |
| 906        | *condicions.* So FP, F, E, B. MS: *condocions.* M: *condicion.* |
| 908        | MS: *Robertus Olyuer est verus . . . ?* is written in a different hand (the end of the line is illegible) in the right margin next to this line. |

|       |                                                                                              |
|-------|----------------------------------------------------------------------------------------------|
|       | *Serge.* M, FP, B: *Serche.* L: *Search.*                                                    |
| 910   | *diverse.* MS: *duerse.* M: *diuerse.* FP: *d[i]uerse.* E: *diuerse.* F, WA: *di[v]erse.* B: *d[i]verse.* |
|       | *transmutacyon.* So FP, E, C, WA. M: *mutacyon.*                                              |
| 912   | *Therefore.* MS: *There fore.* M, FP: *There-fore.*                                          |
|       | *God grant.* So E, L, C. MS: *God.* M, FP: *God [kepe].* F: *God [keep].* WA, B: *God [grant].* |
|       | *misericordiam.* MS: what appears to read *mu* is cancelled before *misericordiam.*          |
| 913   | *pleyferys.* M: *pleseres,* queries *partakers.* FP, F: *pleyseris.* WA, C: *pleyferys.*      |
|       | *angellys.* So E, C, WA. MS: *angell.* M: *angell[es].* FP: *angellis.* B: *angell[ys].*      |
| 914a  | *Fynis.* So M, FP, E. C, WA: omit.                                                            |
|       | MS: in the right margin *nouerint univers* is written in a different hand. Below the text, also in a different hand, is written: *O libere, si quis cui constas forte queretur, / Hyngham, que monacho dices super omnia consto.* (*que*] P *quem*; *consto*] P *consta[s]*) ("O book, if anyone for whom you by chance exist will complain, / Hyngham, whom you will call a monk, exists above all"). |
| after 914a | The bottom two-thirds of this last folio includes upside-down writing, the majority of which is in Latin and is very difficult to read. B$_2$ suggests the following: |

> *Novem tue te Improbitat . . .*
> *Sub monitorem & qui in te nihill se indignum*
> *egit tu tamen vt dure ceruicis puer*
> *effrenius disternere malis liberis vsus ha*
> *bebis quam correctionem quantulum cumque sub ver*

> I trow I was cursyd in my motherys bely or ellys
> I was born [at] a on hapy ower for I can never do thyng
> That men be plesid wyth all now yff I do the best I cann
> oftetymys yt chancyt on hapily I have not
> Knowne a felou so on hapi exsepte the devyll ware
> on hym for evyne now at this tyme I am suer my
> master have two or thre greuys compleyntys on me at
> this tyme yf yt be so my bottkes goo to wreke

> *Mihi non dum edito inprecatam reor infelicitatem*
> *natum me esse me sidere minime dextro relucente*
> *nihill enim vnquam agere quam quod alicui sit cordis Imo*
> *si pro viribus mater rectissimum quod que moliri depis infelici*
> *cor cadet non nolui aliquem a deo infortunatum ama*
> *bo genio ductu persuasum dum hec inpreseintiam*
> *me lumis pluribus me noxiss apud*

> for makyn And off demysent four

# BIBLIOGRAPHY

Aers, David. "*Vox Populi* and the Literature of 1381." In *The Cambridge History of Medieval English Literature*. Ed. David Wallace. Cambridge: Cambridge University Press, 1999. Pp. 432–53.

Alexander, Jonathan J. G. "*Labeur* and *Paresse*: Ideological Representations of Medieval Peasant Labour." *Art Bulletin* 72 (1990), 436–52.

Ashley, Kathleen M. "Titivillus and the Battle of Words in *Mankind*." *Annuale Mediaevale* 16 (1975), 128–50.

Ashley, Kathleen M., and Pamela Sheingorn, eds. *Interpreting Cultural Symbols: Saint Anne in Late Medieval Society*. Athens: University of Georgia Press, 1999.

Axton, Richard. *European Drama of the Early Middle Ages*. London: Hutchinson University Library, 1974.

Baker, Donald C. "The Date of *Mankind*." *Philological Quarterly* 42 (1963), 90–91.

Baker, Margaret. *Folklore and Customs of Rural England*. Newton Abbot: David & Charles, 1988.

Bakhtin, Mikhail. *Rabelais and His World*. Trans. Helene Iswolsky. Bloomington: Indiana University Press, 1984.

Beadle, Richard. "The Scribal Problem in the Macro Manuscript." *English Language Notes* 21 (1984), 1–13.

———. "Monk Thomas Hyngham's Hand in the Macro Manuscript." In *New Science out of Old Books: Studies in Manucripts and Early Printed Books in Honour of A. I. Doyle*. Ed. Richard Beadle and A. J. Piper. Aldershot: Scolar Press, 1995. Pp. 315–41.

Beene, LynnDianne. "Language Patterns in *Mankind*." *Language Quarterly* 21 (1983), 25–29.

Bevington, David. *From Mankind to Marlowe: Growth of Structure in the Popular Drama of Tudor England*. Cambridge, MA: Harvard University Press, 1962.

———, ed. *Medieval Drama*. Boston: Houghton Mifflin, 1975.

Blackburn, Bonnie, and Leofranc Holford-Strevens, eds. *The Oxford Companion to the Year*. Oxford: Oxford University Press, 1999.

Boffey, Julia, and A. S. G. Edwards, eds. *A New Index of Middle English Verse*. London: British Library, 2005.

Brandl, Alois, ed. *Quellen des Weltlichen Dramas in England vor Shakespeare*. Strassburg: Karl J. Trübner, 1898.

Brannen, Anne. "A Century of *Mankind*: How a Very Bad Play Became Good." *Medieval Perspectives* 15 (2000), 11–20.

Brantley, Jessica, and Thomas Fulton. "*Mankind* in a Year without Kings." *Journal of Medieval and Early Modern Studies* 36 (2006), 321–54.

Camille, Michael. "'When Adam Delved': Laboring on the Land in English Medieval Art." In *Agriculture in the Middle Ages: Technology, Practice, and Representation*. Ed. Del Sweeney. Philadelphia: University of Pennsylvania Press, 1995. Pp. 247–76.

*Castle of Perseverance*. In *The Macro Plays*. Ed. Mark Eccles. EETS o.s. 262. London: Oxford University Press, 1969. Pp. 1–112.

Chambers, E. K. *English Literature at the Close of the Middle Ages*. Oxford: Clarendon Press, 1945.

Chambers, Mark. "Physicality, Violence, and the Psychomachia in the Early English Morality Plays." In *Tudor Theatre: Allegory in the Theatre*. Ed. Peter Happé. Bern: Peter Lang, 2000. Pp. 1–20.

————. "Weapons of Conversion: *Mankind* and the Fifteenth-Century Preaching Controversy." *Philological Quarterly* 83 (2004), 1–11.

Chaucer, Geoffrey. *The Riverside Chaucer*. Ed. Larry D. Benson. Boston: Houghton Mifflin, 1987.

Clopper, Lawrence M. "*Mankind* and Its Audience." *Comparative Drama* 8 (1974), 347–55.

Coldewey, John C. "The Non-Cycle Plays and the East Anglian Tradition." In *Cambridge Companion to Medieval English Theatre*. Ed. Richard Beadle. Cambridge: Cambridge University Press, 1994. Pp. 189–210.

————, ed. *Early English Drama: An Anthology*. New York: Garland, 1993.

Coogan, Sister Mary Philippa. *An Interpretation of the Moral Play, Mankind*. Washington, DC: Catholic University of America Press, 1947.

Craig, Hardin. "Morality Plays and Elizabethan Drama." *Shakespeare Quarterly* 1 (1950), 64–72.

————. *English Religious Drama of the Middle Ages*. Oxford: Clarendon Press, 1960.

Davenport, Tony. "'Lusty fresche galaunts.'" In *Aspects of Early English Drama*. Ed. Paula Neuss. Cambridge: D. S. Brewer, 1983. Pp. 110–28.

Davenport, W. A. "Peter Idley and the Devil in *Mankind*." *English Studies* 64 (1983), 106–12.

Dean, James M., ed. *Medieval English Political Writings*. Kalamazoo, MI: Medieval Institute Publications, 1996.

Denny, Neville. "Aspects of the Staging of *Mankind*." *Medium Aevum* 43 (1974), 252–63.

Dickens, Bruce, A. M. Armstrong, A. Mawer, and F. M. Stenton. *The Place-Names of Cumberland*. 3 vols. Cambridge: Cambridge University Press, 1950–53.

*Digby Mary Magdalene*. In *The Digby Plays*. Ed. F. J. Furnivall. EETS o.s. 70. London: Oxford University Press, 1967. Pp. 53–136.

Diller, Hans-Jürgen. "Laughter in Medieval English Drama: A Critique of Modernizing and Historical Analyses." *Comparative Drama* 36 (2002), 1–19.

Dillon, Janette. "*Mankind* and the Politics of 'English Laten.'" *Medievalia et Humanistica* 20 (1994), 41–64.

Eccles, Mark. "The Macro Plays." *Notes and Queries* 31 (1984), 27–29.

————, ed. *The Macro Plays*. EETS o.s. 262. London: Oxford University Press, 1969.

Eisenbichler, Konrad, and Wim Hüsken, eds. *Carnival and the Carnivalesque: The Fool, the Reformer, the Wildman, and Others in Early Modern Theatre*. Amsterdam: Rodopi, 1994.

Epp, Garrett. "The Vicious Guise: Effeminacy, Sodomy, and *Mankind*." In *Becoming Male in the Middle Ages*. Ed. Jeffrey Jerome Cohen and Bonnie Wheeler. New York: Garland, 2000. Pp. 303–20.

*"Everyman" and Its Dutch Original, "Elckerlijc."* Ed. Clifford Davidson, Martin W. Walsh, and Ton J. Broos. Kalamazoo, MI: Medieval Institute Publications, 2007.

Farmer, John S., ed. *Recently Recovered "Lost" Tudor Plays with Some Others*. London: Early English Drama Society, 1907.

Firth, C. B. "Benefit of Clergy in the Time of Edward IV." *English Historical Review* 32 (1917), 175–91.

Fletcher, Alan J. "The Meaning of 'Gostly to Owr Purpos' in *Mankind*." *Notes and Queries* 31 (1984), 301–02.

Forest-Hill, Lynn. "*Mankind* and the Fifteenth-Century Preaching Controversy." *Medieval and Renaissance Drama in England* 15 (2003), 17–42.

Friedman, Albert B. "'When Adam Delved . . .': Contexts of a Historic Proverb." In *The Learned and the Lewed: Studies in Chaucer and Medieval Literature*. Ed. Larry D. Benson. Cambridge, MA: Harvard University Press, 1974. Pp. 213–30.

Furnivall, F. J., and Alfred W. Pollard, eds. *The Macro Plays*. EETS e.s. 91. London: Oxford University Press, 1904. Pp. 1–34.

Gabel, L. C. *Benefit of Clergy in England in the Later Middle Ages*. New York: Octagon Books, 1969.

Galloway, Andrew. "The Making of a Social Ethic in Late-Medieval England: From *Gratitudo* to 'Kyndenesse.'" *Journal of the History of Ideas* 55 (1994), 365–83.

Garner, Stanton B., Jr. "Theatricality in *Mankind* and *Everyman*." *Studies in Philology* 84 (1987), 272–85.

Gash, Anthony. "Carnival against Lent: The Ambivalence of Medieval Drama." In *Medieval Literature: Criticism, Ideology, and History*. Ed. David Aers. New York: St. Martin's Press, 1986. Pp. 74–98.

Gayley, Charles Mills. *Plays of Our Forefathers and Some of the Traditions upon Which They Were Founded.* New York: Duffield and Company, 1907.

Gibson, Gail McMurray. *The Theater of Devotion: East Anglian Drama and Society in the Late Middle Ages.* Chicago: University of Chicago Press, 1989.

Gower, John. *Confessio Amantis.* Ed. Russell A. Peck, with Latin translations by Andrew Galloway. 3 vols. Kalamazoo, MI: Medieval Institute Publications, 2000–06.

Happé, Peter. "The Macro Plays Revisited." *European Medieval Drama* 11 (2008), 37–57.

*Hick Scorner.* In *Two Tudor Interludes: Youth and Hick Scorner.* Ed. Ian Lancashire. Manchester: Manchester University Press, 1980. Pp. 153–238.

Humphrey, Chris. *The Politics of Carnival: Festive Misrule in Medieval England.* Manchester: Manchester University Press, 2001.

Jambeck, Thomas J., and Reuben R. Lee. "'Pope Pokett' and the Date of *Mankind.*" *Mediaeval Studies* 39 (1979), 511–13.

Jennings, Margaret. "Tutivillus: The Literary Career of the Recording Demon." *Studies in Philology* 74 (1977), 1–95.

Justice, Steven. *Writing and Rebellion: England in 1381.* Berkeley: University of California Press, 1994.

Keiller, Mabel M. "The Influence of *Piers Plowman* on the Macro Play of *Mankind.*" *PMLA* 26 (1911), 339–55.

King, Pamela M. "Morality Plays." In *The Cambridge Companion to Medieval English Theatre.* Ed. Richard Beadle. Cambridge: Cambridge University Press, 1994. Pp. 240–64.

Langland, William. *Piers Plowman: A Parallel-Text Edition of the A, B, C and Z Versions.* Ed. A. V. C. Schmidt. London: Longman, 1995.

Lester, G. A., ed. *Three Late Medieval Morality Plays.* London: A & C Black, 1997.

*Lincoln Diocese Documents, 1450–1544.* Ed. A. Clark. EETS o.s. 149. London: Oxford University Press, 1971.

Lydgate, John. *The Minor Poems of John Lydgate: Edited from All Available Manuscripts, with an Attempt to Establish the Lydgate Canon. Part II: Secular Poems.* Ed. Henry Noble MacCracken. EETS o.s. 192. London: Oxford University Press, 1934.

MacKenzie, W. Roy. "A New Source for *Mankind.*" *PMLA* 27 (1912), 98–105.

*The Macro Plays: The Castle of Perseverance, Wisdom, Mankind: A Facsimile Edition with Facing Transcriptions.* Ed. David Bevington. New York: Johnson Reprint Corporation, 1972.

*Mankind.* In Bevington, *Medieval Drama.* Pp. 901–38.

———. In Coldewey, *Early English Drama: An Anthology.* Pp. 105–35.

———. In Eccles, *The Macro Plays.* Pp. xxxvii–xlvi, 153–84, and 216–27.

———. In Farmer, *Recently Recovered "Lost" Tudor Plays with Some Others.* Pp. 1–40.

———. In Furnivall and Pollard, *The Macro Plays.* Pp. 1–34.

———. In Lester, *Three Late Medieval Morality Plays.* Pp. xx–xxv and 1–58.

———. In *The Macro Plays: The Castle of Perseverance, Wisdom, Mankind*, ed. Bevington. Pp. 253–305.

———. In Manly, *Specimens of the Pre-Shakesperean Drama.* Pp. 315–52.

———. In Walker, *Medieval Drama: An Anthology.* Pp. 258–80.

Manly, John Matthews, ed. *Specimens of the Pre-Shakesperean Drama.* Vol. 1. Boston: Ginn, 1897.

Marshall, John. "'O Ye Soverens that Sytt and Ye Brothern that Stonde Ryght Wppe': Addressing the Audiences of *Mankind.*" *European Medieval Drama* 1 (1997), 189–202.

Masri, Heather. "Carnival Laughter in the Pardoner's Tale." *Medieval Perspectives* 10 (1995), 148–56.

"Mundus et Infans." In *Three Late Medieval Morality Plays.* Ed. G. A. Lester. London: A & C Black, 1997. Pp. xxx–xxxvii and 107–57.

Neuss, Paula. "Active and Idle Language: Dramatic Images in *Mankind.*" In *Medieval Drama.* Ed. Neville Denny. London: Edward Arnold, 1973. Pp. 41–67.

*The N-Town Plays.* Ed. Douglas Sugano. Kalamazoo, MI: Medieval Institute Publications, 2007.

"Occupation and Idleness." In *Non-Cycle Plays and the Winchester Dialogues: Facsimiles of Plays and Fragments in Various Manuscripts and the Dialogues in Winchester College MS 33.* Intro. Norman Davis. Leeds: University of Leeds, 1979. Pp. 161–78 and 192–208.

Peterson, Michael T. "*Fragmina Verborum*: The Vices' Use of Language in the Macro Plays." *Florilegium* 9 (1987), 155–67.

Pettitt, Tom. "*Mankind*: An English *Fastnachtspiel?*" In *Festive Drama*. Ed. Meg Twycross. Cambridge: D. S. Brewer, 1996. Pp. 190–202.

Piese, Amanda. "Representing Spiritual Truth in *Mankind* and *Ane Satyre of the Thrie Estaitis*." In *Tudor Theatre: Allegory in the Theatre*. Ed. Peter Happé. Bern: Peter Lang, 2000. Pp. 135–44.

Pineas, Rainer. "The English Morality Play as a Weapon of Religious Controversy." *Studies in English Literature* 2 (1962), 157–80.

Potter, Robert. *The English Morality Play: Origins, History, and Influence of a Dramatic Tradition*. London: Routledge, 1975.

Preston, Michael J. "Re-Presentations of (Im)moral Behavior in the Middle English Non-Cycle Play *Mankind*." In *Folklore, Literature, and Cultural Theory: Collected Essays*. Ed. Cathy Lynn Preston. New York: Garland, 1995. Pp. 214–39.

Price, Amanda. "Dramatizing the Word." *Leeds Studies in English* (1998), 292–303.

Quinn, Esther Casier. *The Quest of Seth for the Oil of Mercy*. Chicago: University of Chicago Press, 1962.

Rastall, Richard. "The Sounds of Hell." In *The Iconography of Hell*. Ed. Clifford Davidson and Thomas H. Seiler. Kalamazoo, MI: Medieval Institute Publications, 1992. Pp. 102–31.

Reaney, P. H. *A Dictionary of British Surnames*. London: Routledge and K. Paul, 1958.

Robertson, Kellie. *The Laborer's Two Bodies: Labor and the "Work" of the Text in Medieval Britain, 1350–1500*. New York: Palgrave Macmillan, 2006.

Rossiter, A. P. *English Drama from Early Times to the Elizabethans*. London: Hutchinson, 1950.

Salzman, L. F., ed. *The Victoria History of the County of Cambridge and the Isle of Ely*. Vol. 2. London: Oxford University Press, 1948.

Scherb, Victor I. *Staging Faith: East Anglian Drama in the Later Middle Ages*. Madison, NJ: Fairleigh Dickinson University Press, 2001.

Sikorska, Liliana. "*Mankind* and the Question of Power Dynamics: Some Remarks on the Validity of Sociolinguistic Reading." *Neuphilologische Mitteilungen* 97 (1996), 201–16.

Skelton, John. *John Skelton: The Complete English Poems*. Ed. John Scattergood. New Haven, CT: Yale University Press, 1983.

Smart, W. K. *Some English and Latin Sources for the Morality of Wisdom*. Mensha, WI: George Banta Publishing, 1912.

———. "Some Notes on *Mankind*." *Modern Philology* 14 (1916–17), 45–58 and 293–313.

———. "*Mankind* and the Mumming Plays." *Modern Language Notes* (1917), 21–25.

Smith, William G., and F. P. Wilson, eds. *Oxford Dictionary of English Proverbs*. Oxford: Clarendon Press, 1970.

Sponsler, Claire. *Drama and Resistance: Bodies, Goods, and Theatricality in Late Medieval England*. Minneapolis: University of Minnesota Press, 1997.

Stechow, Wolfgang. *Pieter Brueghel the Elder*. New York: Harry N. Abrams, 1969.

Stock, Lorraine Kochanske. "The Thematic and Structural Unity of *Mankind*." *Studies in Philology* 72 (1975), 386–407.

Teversham, T. F. *A History of the Village of Sawston*. 2 vols. Sawston: Crompton and Son, 1942–45.

Thundy, Zacharias P. "Morality Plays: *Mankind* and *Everyman*." In *Old and Middle English Literature*. Ed. Jeffrey Helterman and Jerome Mitchell. Detroit: Gale, 1994. Pp. 400–04.

Tilley, Morris Palmer. *A Dictionary of the Proverbs in England in the Sixteenth and Seventeenth Centuries*. Ann Arbor: University of Michigan Press, 1950.

*The Towneley Plays*. Ed. Alfred W. Pollard. EETS e.s. 71. London: Oxford University Press, 1973.

———. Ed. Martin Stevens and A. C. Cawley. 2 vols. EETS s.s. 13–14. Oxford: Oxford University Press, 1994.

Twycross, Meg. "The Theatricality of Medieval English Plays." In *The Cambridge Companion to Medieval English Theatre*. Ed. Richard Beadle. Cambridge: Cambridge University Press, 1994. Pp. 37–84.

Twycross, Meg, and Sarah Carpenter. *Masks and Masking in Medieval and Early Tudor England*. Aldershot: Ashgate, 2002.

Walker, Greg, ed. *Medieval Drama: An Anthology*. Oxford: Blackwell, 2000.

Watkins, John. "The Allegorical Theatre: Moralities, Interludes, and Protestant Drama." In *The Cambridge History of Medieval English Literature*. Ed. David Wallace. Cambridge: Cambridge University Press, 1999. Pp. 77–92.

Wedgwood, J. C. *History of Parliament: Biographies of the Members of the Commons' House, 1439–1509*. London: Stationary Office, 1936.

Whiting, Bartlett Jere, with the collaboration of Helen Wescott Whiting. *Proverbs, Sentences, and Proverbial Phrases from English Writings Mainly before 1500*. Cambridge, MA: The Belknap Press of Harvard University Press, 1968.

Wickham, Glynne. *English Moral Interludes*. London: Dent, 1976.

Williams, Arnold. *The Drama of Medieval England*. East Lansing: Michigan State University Press, 1961.

*Wisdom*. In *The Macro Plays*. Ed. Mark Eccles. EETS o.s. 262. London: Oxford University Press, 1969. Pp. 113–52.

Woolf, Rosemary. *The English Mystery Plays*. Berkeley: University of California Press, 1972.

Wyclif, John. *Select English Works of John Wyclif*. Ed. Thomas Arnold. Vol. 3. Oxford: Clarendon Press, 1871.

*Youth*. In *Two Tudor Interludes: Youth and Hick Scorner*. Ed. Ian Lancashire. Manchester: Manchester Univeristy Press, 1980. Pp. 99–152.

*Stanzaic Guy of Warwick*, edited by Alison Wiggins (2004)

*Saints' Lives in Middle English Collections*, edited by E. Gordon Whatley, with Anne B. Thompson and Robert K. Upchurch (2004)

*Siege of Jerusalem*, edited by Michael Livingston (2004)

*The Kingis Quair and Other Prison Poems*, edited by Linne R. Mooney and Mary-Jo Arn (2005)

*The Chaucerian Apocrypha: A Selection*, edited by Kathleen Forni (2005)

John Gower, *The Minor Latin Works*, edited and translated by R. F. Yeager, with *In Praise of Peace*, edited by Michael Livingston (2005)

*Sentimental and Humorous Romances: Floris and Blancheflour, Sir Degrevant, The Squire of Low Degree, The Tournament of Tottenham, and The Feast of Tottenham*, edited by Erik Kooper (2006)

*The Dicts and Sayings of the Philosophers*, edited by John William Sutton (2006)

*Everyman and Its Dutch Original, Elckerlijc*, edited by Clifford Davidson, Martin W. Walsh, and Ton J. Broos (2007)

*The N-Town Plays*, edited by Douglas Sugano, with assistance by Victor I. Scherb (2007)

*The Book of John Mandeville*, edited by Tamarah Kohanski and C. David Benson (2007)

John Lydgate, *The Temple of Glas*, edited by J. Allan Mitchell (2007)

*The Northern Homily Cycle*, edited by Anne B. Thompson (2008)

*Codex Ashmole 61: A Compilation of Popular Middle English Verse*, edited by George Shuffelton (2008)

*Chaucer and the Poems of "Ch,"* edited by James I. Wimsatt (revised edition 2009)

William Caxton, *The Game and Playe of the Chesse*, edited by Jenny Adams (2009)

John the Blind Audelay, *Poems and Carols*, edited by Susanna Fein (2009)

*Two Moral Interludes: The Pride of Life and Wisdom*, edited by David Klausner (2009)

John Lydgate, *Mummings and Entertainments*, edited by Claire Sponsler (2010)


## COMMENTARY SERIES

Haimo of Auxerre, *Commentary on the Book of Jonah*, translated with an introduction and notes by Deborah Everhart (1993)

*Medieval Exegesis in Translation: Commentaries on the Book of Ruth*, translated with an introduction and notes by Lesley Smith (1996)

*Nicholas of Lyra's Apocalypse Commentary*, translated with an introduction and notes by Philip D. W. Krey (1997)

Rabbi Ezra Ben Solomon of Gerona, *Commentary on the Song of Songs and Other Kabbalistic Commentaries*, selected, translated, and annotated by Seth Brody (1999)

John Wyclif, *On the Truth of Holy Scripture*, translated with an introduction and notes by Ian Christopher Levy (2001)

*Second Thessalonians: Two Early Medieval Apocalyptic Commentaries*, introduced and translated by Steven R. Cartwright and Kevin L. Hughes (2001)

*The "Glossa Ordinaria" on the Song of Songs*, translated with an introduction and notes by Mary Dove (2004)

*The Seven Seals of the Apocalypse: Medieval Texts in Translation*, translated with an introduction and notes by Francis X. Gumerlock (2009)


## DOCUMENTS OF PRACTICE SERIES

*Love and Marriage in Late Medieval London*, selected, translated, and introduced by Shannon McSheffrey (1995)

*Sources for the History of Medicine in Late Medieval England*, selected, introduced, and translated by Carole Rawcliffe (1995)

*A Slice of Life: Selected Documents of Medieval English Peasant Experience*, edited, translated, and with an introduction by Edwin Brezette DeWindt (1996)

*Regular Life: Monastic, Canonical, and Mendicant "Rules,"* selected and introduced by Douglas J. McMillan and Kathryn Smith Fladenmuller (1997); second edition, selected and introduced by Daniel Marcel La Corte and Douglas J. McMillan (2004)

*Women and Monasticism in Medieval Europe: Sisters and Patrons of the Cistercian Reform*, selected, translated, and with an introduction by Constance H. Berman (2002)

*Medieval Notaries and Their Acts: The 1327–1328 Register of Jean Holanie*, introduced, edited, and translated by Kathryn L. Reyerson and Debra A. Salata (2004)

Typeset in 10/13 New Baskerville
and Golden Cockerel Ornaments display
Designed by Linda K. Judy
Manufactured by Cushing-Malloy, Inc.

Medieval Institute Publications
College of Arts and Sciences
Western Michigan University
1903 W. Michigan Avenue
Kalamazoo, MI 49008-5432
http://wmich.edu/medievalpublications

 WESTERN MICHIGAN UNIVERSITY

PGIL2023USA